FAMILIES UNDER STRESS

TONY MANOCCHIO

WILLIAM PETITT

Centre for Therapeutic Communication
London

FAMILIES UNDER STRESS

A psychological interpretation

Routledge & Kegan Paul
London and Boston

First published in 1975
by Routledge & Kegan Paul Ltd
Broadway House, 68–74 Carter Lane,
London EC4V 5EL and
9 Park Street,
Boston, Mass. 02108, USA
Set in Monotype Imprint
and printed in Great Britain by
The Camelot Press Ltd, Southampton
Copyright Tony Manocchio and William Petitt 1975

ISBN 0 7100 8176 6

CONTENTS

CONTENTS

ACKNOWLEDGMENTS

We wish to express our acknowledgments to the following people:

To Mary Young who gave us a number of suggestions regarding choice of plays which might be used. To Mr William Mckenzie, student of English literature, who gave us many ideas about the Hamlet family. To Mr Mike Wibberley who called our attention to the pertinent paragraphs in *Women in Love* and Thomas More. To Mr Kurt Palsvig, Danish psychologist, who read our first draft and gave valuable suggestions on the Hamlet story. To Mr Paul Kastning, who called our attention to the inscription on Hamlet's grave. Finally, to our secretary Erica De'Ath for her help, energy and patience which made life a lot easier for all of us.

We are grateful to the following for permission to quote from copyright material: Dr Jan Van Loewen Ltd for *The Winslow Boy* by Terence Rattigan; Tavistock Publications Ltd, Pantheon Books (a division of Random House Inc.) and the Canadian Broadcasting Corporation for *The Politics of the Family* by R. D. Laing; Viking Press Inc. for *Death of a Salesman* by Arthur Miller; Herbert Kohl and Victor Gollancz Ltd for *Thirty-Six Children*; Jonathan Cape Ltd and Atheneum Publications Inc. for *A Delicate Balance* by Edward Albee; Yale University for *Long Day's Journey into Night* by Eugene O'Neill.

INTRODUCTION

The family. The very word will conjure up a variety of different images and feelings in each person. This is because for each of us our past and present experience of family life is different – some happy, some unhappy; some joyful, some miserable. But the family remains the most important single institution in the lives of most people. It is here that we turn for comfort and assistance – no matter how disorganized or erratic it may be. Robert Frost captures this importance: 'Home is the place where, when you have to go there, they have to take you in.'[1]

Everyone is, or has been, the member of a family at one time or another. This book is about six families. More specifically, it is about the communication that takes place in these families. It was once said that the psychologist William James was a good novelist, and that his brother Henry was a brilliant psychologist. The story may be apocryphal, but its point is well made. Psychology, as a relatively new discipline, has had an influence on most areas of society. A reciprocal influence is most clearly observable in the arts, particularly in literature. For this reason, literature is a treasure house for the psychologist or psychiatrist. And the riches are plundered freely: the classic example is how Freud used the myth of Oedipus to explain succinctly one of his major ideas.

Conjoint family therapy, as a treatment model, concerns itself solely with the communication between family members. This model allows the therapist to approach the family in a special way. He does not attempt to zero in to any special problem and attempt to solve it. Rather he attempts to teach the family a 'new language' through which they should be able to solve each problem as it emerges. The communication's the thing. Every effort is made to encourage and teach the individual family member to express himself openly and honestly at all times to everyone else in the family. It is hoped, in this way, that pain in the family will be reduced as each member learns to express himself in a more positive and constructive fashion.

Thus what is important is the dialogue that takes place between the family members. Not so much what the problem is, but how they tackle it. It is here that we can learn from drama. The basic medium of the playwright is words. The plays that we have selected for this book, we feel, actually demonstrate and illuminate all the issues that we discuss.

There is a strong precedent for our approach, particularly in the field of communication theory. A brief survey of the field reveals some very interesting examples.

Sander in an article (1970) points out that T. S. Eliot's *The Cocktail Party* anticipated the beginnings of family therapy. The psychiatrist in the play is faced with the treatment issues of a family rather than the individual person. In 'Treating the *Doll's House* Marriage', Pittman and Flomenhaft (1970) describe the kind of marriage in Ibsen's play to see how it fits with thirty couples they had in treatment with a five-year follow-up. They point out that few *Doll's House* marriages collapse under their own weight and that they often remain intact, but pathologically so, because one spouse must remain incompetent so that the other partner may survive.

Another example of the use of family therapy analysis and literature is again Ibsen's *Ghosts*. In 'A Re-appraisal of Ibsen's *Ghosts*' Derek Russell Davis (1970) looks at this nineteenth-century social conscience play as a treatment case, complete with diagnosis. Basically, it is the story of a crisis in the relationship between son and mother.

In 'A Nurse, a Family and The Velveteen Rabbit' (Tescher, 1971) the therapist uses a fairy tale to examine the family process in a first interview. She notes how the family members, like the characters in the story, express a wish to become 'real'.

The theatre, too, is used as an illustration. Kantnor and Hoffman (1966) examine parallels between Brechtian theatre and family therapy. They examine the idea of distancing and how it can be used to promote and protect change-producing activity.

In *Identity, Youth and Crisis* (1968), Erik Erikson writes about Hamlet's identity confusion. And finally, communication experts Watzlawick, Beavin and the late Don Jackson (1968) devote a whole chapter to an analysis of the famous American play, *Who's Afraid of Virginia Woolf*.

The pattern that we have followed in this book is as follows: each chapter is based on an analysis of a major play, apart from the first chapter, where we have used two plays. We have selected each play for a particular reason, in that it best demonstrates certain elements of family theory. Chapter 2 is devoted to *Hamlet*. Here we discuss covert communication, the double-bind, the perfect family myth, scapegoating and, finally, secrets and their effects upon the family.

Chapter 3 is based upon *Long Day's Journey into Night* by Eugene O'Neill. This play is particularly appropriate for the study of the closed family system. The major areas that we examine within this system are overt communication and how it is used to maintain closure, and the idea of the 'blame frame'. In examining the Tyrones, we also discover how agreements, when taken to a certain extent, lead to a kind of conspiracy, the purpose of which is to avoid open, painful conflict. Finally we use this tormented family to discuss alternatives for growth – alternatives which this family might have followed if their communication had been better.

The next chapter is largely devoted to the Loman family in *Death of a Salesman* by Arthur Miller. We begin with a brief discussion of the work role, which is particularly important in Western culture. This is followed by discussions of expectations, differentness, fantasy, and the model child. We also reintroduce the idea of secrets in a family, as this is a very important area.

In chapter 5 we meet Edward Albee's family in his play *A Delicate Balance*. In examining this family, we look at the themes of pain, decision-making, roles and survival.

The first chapter has a slightly different format. We look at two families in crisis, who, in contrast to the other families we have met, communicate in a healthy way. The first family are the Winslows, in Terence Rattigan's play *The Winslow Boy*. Our discussion centres around the ideas of decision-making, crisis, communication, physical health in family life, and the open family system.

Our second family was selected for a special reason, for no discussion of the communication in any family is complete unless we examine how it is possible to deal with tragedy. In Synge's play *Riders to the Sea* we discuss something which we all ultimately have to face – how a family deals with the death of one of its members.

At one time the family unit was considered to be a sacred institution, not to be questioned or attacked. Today the concept of the family is being seriously questioned. One of its foremost critics, Dr David Cooper – the *enfant terrible* of British psychiatry and author of *Death of the Family* – states that the family as we know it is finished. He says that modern-day families do not give children enough individuality, that we must find new ways of rearing children.

It is not our aim in this book to question whether or not the family should survive. Our purpose is to examine patterns of communication in both disturbed and healthy families in an attempt to shed some light onto the problems which most families share, no matter what their form.

It has long been established that good mental health is closely related to good relationships within the entire society. In this connection it is worthwhile to note that until recently the tendency was for family specialists to view the nuclear family as an insular unit existing in its own vacuum. However, case histories and practice in family therapy indicate that grandparents are important figures in transmitting pathology from one generation to another. This self-imposed limitation in the treatment field partly explains how the myth developed that 'mental illness' was genetically transmitted. What happened of course was that each succeeding generation of children learned disturbed ways of behaving from their parents before them. In this way such behaviour patterns were perpetuated.

When we discuss the family, and consider the criticisms levelled against it, we must be aware of the great changes which have occurred over the past half century. These changes have affected the family in a number of different and profound ways. In this period we have seen the number of children per family lessened considerably; the role of the woman in society has dramatically altered – and still is altering, as eloquently attested to by the women's liberation movement. Parental roles may be reversed. A recent movement is aimed at establishing once and for all that to have children is a matter of choice – that there is no stigma attached to the childless marriage. Not only are the concepts of marriage and nuclear family being challenged, but new ideas are being actively explored as alternatives – the collective, the network family, the community family, this latter often being based on the ideal of sharing most things – work, parental responsibility and sex.

The extended family has also undergone much revision. The positions of the grandfather, grandmother, aunts and uncles and cousins as members of the family unit no longer have the same meanings for us, especially in the West, as they had even fifty years ago. This is particularly true of the old folks, whom we may shuttle off to old peoples' homes, to hospitals, or even, as the Americans call it, to a 'retirement village'. In this way the young avoid the burden of having them around. In the West it seems we do not value the wisdom of the aged.

We can get a different picture of the part the extended family can play if we look at other cultures. In present-day China, for example, the situation is very different. A recent social work journal stated that when a person becomes mentally ill in that country, he is encouraged to go to hospital, where both the nuclear family and the extended family gather around to offer support and warmth. The person is not treated like a scapegoat by the family or the hospital. This attitude extends even to employment, where the person's job will be held open for his return.

In Yugoslavia too we discover that it is not uncommon for members of three generations to live together under the same roof. While it is true that in part this may be connected with the housing shortage, this is obviously not the whole reason. It is also important to recognize and acknowledge that the extended family members have some important things to pass on to the younger generation.

Thus we can see that the way in which people lead their social lives has undergone a great change. This change has been paralleled by the emergence of a number of very different ideas in therapy. Family therapy is part of this revolution in the treatment field.

Conjoint family therapy as a mode of treatment is very young. It first emerged in the mid-1950s in America, particularly in California. It has had no time to develop traditions. This also means that there is comparatively little research done, and although the research which has been done is more than competent[2] one cannot say at this point that there is any definite evidence to suggest that a breakdown in communication *causes* mental illness; however, what can be stated is that disturbed behaviour is always accompanied by destructive and confusing patterns of communication. This lack of certainty is not due to lack of investigation. Scientific research takes time; and since the mid-1950s an enormous amount of work has been done, as Peter Sedgwick so accurately describes (1972):

> The pathology of family communication has become one of the great research enterprises of American science. Hundreds of families have trooped into the laboratories of academic institutes and hospitals, there to have their entire verbal output tape-recorded over many sessions, their gestures and eyemovements filmed, and their biographies unearthed in depth by interdisciplinary panels of doctors, psychologists, sociologists and technicians. The families inhabit this select theatre for a period of hours or days, enacting a kind of real-life TV serial based on their usual domestic interchange, and then depart. They leave behind them a mass of sound tracks, videotapes, behaviour checklists, completed test-sheets and other revelatory material, a huge deposit of past praxis which is then worked over for months by the bureau of investigators, and in due course delivered to the interested public as a journal article. The cumulative bibliography of the Schizophrenic Family forms a veritable saga of modern home-life, running in repeated instalments through some half-dozen scholarly channels over about fifteen years, and with no end-point in sight.

Traditionally, when a family member exhibited disturbed behaviour, it seemed appropriate for the therapist to see the person by himself, in just the same way in which a medical doctor might see his patient. Thus the disturbed person was completely isolated from the family system. The idea was to treat the person who had been identified as 'sick' in a hospital or in a private, one-to-one therapy. Once the symptoms had disappeared he was returned to his social milieu. The model, primarily a psycho-analytical one, was in great vogue until the mid-1950s (and still is in many quarters). Using this model, the clinician helped the patient to resolve his unconscious conflicts by helping him to gain 'insight', the all-powerful, magical word which could explain everything.

Happily, since the Second World War, the family treatment picture has undergone a considerable change. In the mid-1950s, a great deal of writing and some fairly sophisticated research was produced by the Mental Research Institute at Palo Alto, California. Under the guidance of anthropologist Gregory Bateson and doctors Jay Haley and the late Don Jackson, a number of theories were developed which help us to look at communications within the family as a complete system.

Important breakthroughs in science often seem to occur almost by accident. (Witness the discovery of penicillin by Dr Alexander Fleming in 1928, as an example of this.) The same, seemingly accidental, discovery occurred at Palo Alto which was to give birth to the idea that there is a relationship between patterns of communication amongst family members and the emergence of the schizophrenic individual. Whilst studying communication patterns in a particular family which they had in treatment, the scientists became intrigued as to why the patient could not tolerate the presence of the parents for longer than a few minutes without collapsing. What they observed changed their views so radically that within a year they had developed a systematic programme for the treatment of schizophrenics. Within this systematic programme were incorporated such famous concepts as the double-bind and the scapegoat syndrome which had been with us for a long time without being a part of a unified theory of family therapy.

Within a decade a number of people emerged who had developed specific techniques and philosophies which enabled them to treat the complete family rather than the individual. (Among the most important people were, in America, Weakland, Bateson, Jackson, Watzlawick, Haley and Satir, and in England, Laing and Esterson.) Within this book we shall remain fairly strictly with one such model – that of conjoint family therapy (or communication theory) as developed by Mrs Virginia Satir.

Mrs Satir has spent all of her professional life trying to get families to communicate more clearly by giving clear messages rather than confused ones. She has worked tirelessly not only to help families to get better understanding of themselves but she has also trained thousands of workers in the field in an attempt to make some sense out of the many complications that arise when one attempts to look at a family in a therapeutic way.

Today the idea of treating the entire family at the same time is an accepted mode of treatment in most Western countries. The importance of this change can be realized when we remember that it was only a few years ago that it was only radical or courageous clinicians who would dare to bring the family together, or even the couple for a discussion of marital problems. The value of seeing the whole family together can be perceived in the following example.

Dr Tom Main, one of Britain's leading psychiatrists and the head of the Cassel Hospital in Richmond, Surrey, states categorically that often the 'patient' is not really the one who is sick but it is the family that is sick. At the Cassel, an attempt is made to preserve the mother-child relationship by admitting both and if at all possible the father too is admitted. One mother tried to palm off her child on Dr Main by saying 'take my child, she's a problem and I can't do anything with her'. He took one look at the mother and said he would treat them as a family unit. As it turned out, the mother was the one with the most severe problems.

The development of a communication theory that can be applied to families is part of a much wider movement that has grown enormously in stature since the Second World War. This seems a logical progression for our lives depend on clear communication. We hope that by writing this book we have made a meaningful contribution to the advancement of clear communication.

Notes

1 Robert Frost, *Death of the Hired Man*.
2 Two examples of research are Bateson, Jackson, Haley and Weakland (1956), also Laing and Esterson (1964). For those interested, a comprehensive review of family theories is Mishler and Waxler (1968).

1 TWO FAMILIES

Introduction

In the following chapters we will look at patterns of disturbed communication. At this point we feel it would be valuable to examine the way a 'healthy' family behaves. In much the same way as Maslow, the authors feel that to content themselves with the discussion of pathological symptoms is to lose sight of the whole picture. Health is a dynamic drive, as is sickness – we can learn at least as much from healthy people as unhealthy ones.

This is a problem faced by the therapist – he is usually called in only at a time of crisis. If we pursue this line of thought, we might see society as a family that only has mediocre expectations for its children – as long as they stay out of trouble and conform to certain standards, then everything is fine. We make very little attempt to work with the individual's potential.

If we think about industry for a moment we can see this idea exemplified. Very often change can only be brought about by the precipitation of a crisis or occasionally the other way round. This is like saying 'We will stay as we are until it is no longer possible'. If we indulge our fantasies for a moment, we might see that it is possible to have a different dominant ethic; one which would encourage every individual to attempt to live at the highest level possible. The ethic might be 'We will continue to strive for different means of expression and self-fulfilment'. This is the way a good family therapist must work: he would strive to use a health model rather than a disease model. His primary expectation would be that everyone has the potential for growth. He will strive for the closed family to become more open, the affectionless family to become more loving, for the rigid and uncompromising family to allow for differences.

The authors have been among the loudest complainants that too often the social scientist falls for the myth that his subject is value-free. By so doing he perpetuates the fantasy of the 'truly objective' social scientist who is 'morally neutral' and the 'completely impartial' observer. When we carry this idea of objectivity to its natural conclusion in the social sciences the results are terrifying. Roszak captures them very well (1968):

> I can perceive no more than your behavioural façades. I can grant you no more reality or psychic coherence than this perception allows. I shall observe this behaviour of yours and record it. I shall not enter into your life, your task, your condition of existents. Do not turn to me or appeal to me or ask me to become involved with you. I am here only as a temporary observer whose role is to stand back and record and later to make sense of what you seem to be doing or intending. I assume that I can adequately understand what you are doing or intending without entering wholly into your life. I am not particularly interested in what you uniquely are; I am interested only in the general pattern to which you conform. I assume I have the right to use you to perform this process of classification. I assume I have the right to reduce all that you are to an integer in my science.

Inherent in the theory of family therapy that we are discussing in this book are a number of values. It is posited that it is important that the family possess certain qualities or values if its members are to achieve maximum growth potential. These qualities include the open display of feeling – which includes the sharing of such opposite emotions as extreme anger or love. The individual must feel free enough to act spontaneously and talk honestly. This automatically precludes secrets or taboos, as these place limits on the interaction of members. Taboos are difficult as these are culturally determined – for example death and incest. But the question 'Why' remains – cultural mores do change.

A further value inherent in this model is that people are allowed to be different. This is one of the more helpful ways in which the individual can be encouraged to find self-expression and realize his own identity. Allowing and encouraging family members to be different has certain consequences. This assumes that independence and its corollary self-responsibility will be encouraged and stressed.

It is important that we have high expectations in all areas. If we agree that no one is working at their fullest potential then it is not unreasonable to assume that they can do better than they are doing. This principle must also operate in families, if members are to grow.

The Winslow family: *The Winslow Boy* by Terence Rattigan

List of characters

Ronnie Winslow	John Watherstone
Arthur Winslow	Desmond Curry
Grace Winslow	Miss Barnes
Dickie Winslow	Fred
Catherine Winslow	Sir Robert Morton
Violet	

Synopsis of the plot of the play

Ronnie Winslow, fourteen years old, is expelled from Naval Cadet Training School after being found guilty by secret Court Martial of stealing a five-shilling postal order. His father refuses to accept the verdict of guilty, but fails in any attempt to make the inquiry public.

In attempting to clear his son's name, the father embarks on a social crusade. It is a long battle, lasting almost two years. Most of the family money is lost, the daughter loses her fiancé because of pressure of public ridicule, and the eldest son is forced to leave university. The father, too, pays a heavy price, for his health rapidly deteriorates.

But the son is finally cleared and thus the family sacrifices take on a greater meaning, for in this legal reversal on the part of the Navy is contained the whole myth of David and Goliath, an enormous societal triumph gained by such a small but resolute and strong group of people.

The proud family

The Winslow family is at once both very ordinary and extremely remarkable. In their war with the State they have many personal battles which have to be triumphed in. The ordinariness is in their feelings for each other, the way they talk, the beliefs they hold. The extraordinariness they possess lies in the fact that they live their values, and fight for their beliefs.

It is not hard to believe that the family grows closer in a tolerance and understanding of itself as the months drag on. For at no time is the impossible or the impractical course demanded; here is merely the resolute pursual of an eminently reasonable but difficult goal. For no one in this family is coerced or gagged or even confused by what is happening. There is a clarity, even in the suffering of each individual.

But of course there is a price. In every battle soldiers must die. And while the individual has to face later decisions – which will hopefully be forever – there will have to be a restricting and some voluntary giving up of some valued alternatives. Such battles can never be easy, and should not be. But it is maybe only in such battles, voluntarily but firmly accepted, that the human spirit is tempered.

We trace four major themes in this section: decision-making, crisis, communication, and a new and very important topic, that of the relationship between physical and mental health. We close this section with a discussion of the open family system.

Decision-making

The major decision in the Winslow family is a unilateral one – and all else follows from this first decision. Bearing in mind the historical material we have already discussed, this could have been a quite normal state of affairs for the time. The young son Ronnie, age fourteen, returns from Naval School unexpectedly. He has been dismissed after being charged and found guilty of stealing a five-shilling postal order. The family fights the case, but it would seem a pretty safe assumption that the final decision was made by the father. His decision is motivated by two factors – the belief in his son's innocence and a strong sense of social justice.

Once committed to the decision the consequences are pretty drastic. The eldest son has to leave college, the family finances are severely depleted, the daughter loses her fiancé, and the father's health is undermined. Only at one point is there talk of dropping the case. This is an important point because it gives us great insight into the qualities of the relationships in this family. A letter arrives whilst the father, Catherine and Sir Robert, the barrister, are discussing the case. After reading it the father drops a bombshell:

SIR ROBERT We were discussing how to proceed with the case –

ARTHUR The case? (*He stares, a little blankly, from one to the other.*) Yes. We must think of that, mustn't we? (*Pause.*) How to proceed with the case? (*To Sir Robert, abruptly.*) I'm afraid I don't think, all things considered, that much purpose will be served by going on –

(*Sir Robert and Catherine stare at him blankly. Catherine goes quickly to him and snatches the letter from his lap. She begins to read.*)

SIR ROBERT (*with a sudden change of tone*) Of course we must go on.

ARTHUR (*in a low voice*) It is not for you to choose, Sir. The choice is mine.

SIR ROBERT (*harshly*) Then you must reconsider it. To give up now would be insane.

ARTHUR Insane? My sanity has already been called in question tonight – for carrying the case as far as I have.

SIR ROBERT Whatever the contents of that letter, or whatever has happened to make you lose heart, I insist that we continue the fight –

ARTHUR Insist? We? It is my fight – my fight alone – and it is for me alone to judge when the time has come to give it up. . . .

CATHERINE My father doesn't mean what he says, Sir Robert.

SIR ROBERT I am glad to hear it.

CATHERINE Perhaps I should explain this letter –

ARTHUR No, Kate.

CATHERINE Sir Robert knows so much about our family affairs, Father, I don't see it will matter much if he learns a little more. (*To Sir Robert.*) This letter is from a certain Colonel Watherstone who is the father of the man I am engaged to. He goes on to say that unless my father will give him a firm undertaking to drop this whining and reckless agitation – I suppose he means the case – he will exert every bit of influence he has over his son to prevent him marrying me.

SIR ROBERT   I see. An ultimatum.

CATHERINE   Yes – but a pointless one.

SIR ROBERT   Your daughter seems prepared to take the risk –

ARTHUR   I am not. Not, at least, until I know how great a risk it is –

SIR ROBERT   How do you estimate the risk, Miss Winslow? (*Pause. Catherine, for all her bravado, is plainly scared. She is engaged in lighting a cigarette as Sir Robert asks his question.*)

CATHERINE (*at length*)   Negligible.

(pp. 69–71)

The father is prepared to drop the case for the sake of his daughter, he is not prepared to sacrifice her happiness. She, on her part, is remarkably level-headed and clear, and is obviously prepared to risk her engagement for the sake of what she believes is right. As we see later, her fiancé does in fact break off the engagement because of the case and all its publicity. The price that the Winslow family pays is indeed a heavy one.

To make decisions we have to be clear about what our priorities are. Shortly after the fight to clear Ronnie's name is begun, money becomes rather tight. Some economies have to be made. One of them directly involves Dickie, the eldest son, who is a university student. (At this period of time, students had to pay their own college fees and expenses.) The father opens the discussion:

ARTHUR   Very well. (*He stares at him for a moment.*) What do you suppose one of your book-maker friends would lay in the way of odds against your getting a degree?

(*Pause.*)

DICKIE   Oh, well, let's think. Say – about evens.

ARTHUR   Hm. I rather doubt if at that price your friends would find many takers.

DICKIE   Well – perhaps seven to four against.

ARTHUR   I see. And what about the odds against your
  eventually becoming a Civil Servant?
DICKIE   Well – a bit steeper, I suppose.
ARTHUR   Exactly. Quite a bit steeper.
(*Pause.*)
DICKIE   You don't want to have a bet, do you?
ARTHUR   No, Dickie. I'm not a gambler. And that's exactly
  the trouble. Unhappily I am no longer in a position to
  gamble two hundred pounds a year on what you yourself
  admit is an outside chance. . . . You can finish your second
  year.
DICKIE   And what then?
ARTHUR   I can get you a job in the Bank.
DICKIE (*quietly*)   Oh Lord! . . .

ARTHUR   I'm afraid this is rather a shock for you. I'm sorry.
DICKIE   What? No, No, it isn't really. I've been rather
  expecting it, as a matter of fact – especially since I have
  heard you are hoping to brief Sir Robert Morton.

(pp. 39–40)

There are a couple of interesting points about this decision.
The first is that it is made by the father and communicated to
Dickie. At the beginning of the play, we had heard that Dickie
had not been doing very well at college – had done very little work
and had failed his exam. With the need to call in a top flight
lawyer, money becomes a top priority in the family. Dickie
accepts this, and, in fact, almost seems relieved at the decision. It
seems doubtful that he ever would have made a good student.
This decision, as well as being discussed openly, allows for difference in the family, in that the father loses no respect for his son
as he is such a bad student.

Catherine and her fiancé, John, are talking about the case.
John's father, a retired Colonel, has informed the Winslow
family that if they persist with the case and if his son still wishes
to marry Catherine, then his allowance will be cut off. The money
is very important to John, and he suggests to Catherine that it
would be better if the case were dropped:

JOHN (*cautiously*)   Well – I think you should consider it very
  carefully before you take the next step –

CATHERINE I can assure you we will, John. The question is –
what *is* the next step?

JOHN Well – this is the way I see it. I'm going to be honest
now. I hope you don't mind –

CATHERINE No. I should welcome it.

JOHN Your young brother over there pinches or doesn't
pinch a five-bob postal order. For over a year you and your
father fight a magnificent fight on his behalf, and I'm sure
that everyone admires you for it –

CATHERINE Your father hardly seems to –

JOHN Well, he's a die-hard. And now, good heavens, you've
had the whole damned House of Commons getting
themselves worked up to a frenzy about it. Surely, darling,
that's enough for you? My God! Surely the case can end
there?

(p. 74)

Catherine is here faced with two major alternatives. If she drops
the case, she will have her dowry, her fiancé will keep his allowance, and they will be sure to be married. But she will have to face
her family, and her own conscience. If she insists that the case
goes on, she is taking a great risk of losing John, whom she loves.
Catherine is strong-willed, a woman of great principle. In an age
before women really had the right to vote, she was devoting a
great deal of her energies to the Labour Movement and the
Suffragettes. She sees her brother's case as a matter of principle.
As such it is of great importance to her:

CATHERINE Yes, I suppose the case can end there.

JOHN (*pointing to Ronnie*) *He* won't mind.

CATHERINE No, I know he won't.

JOHN Look at him! Perfectly happy and content. Not a care
in the world. How do you know what's going on in his
mind? How can you be so sure that he didn't do it?

CATHERINE (*also gazing down at Ronnie*) I'm not so sure he
didn't do it.

JOHN (*appalled*) Good Lord! Then why in Heaven's name
have you and your father spent all this time and money
trying to prove his innocence?

CATHERINE His innocence or guilt isn't important to me.
They are to my father. All that I care about is that people

should know that a Government Department has ignored a fundamental human right and that it should be forced to acknowledge it. That's all that's important to me.

JOHN   But, darling, after all those long noble words, it does really resolve itself to a question of a fourteen-year-old kid and a five-bob postal order, doesn't it?

CATHERINE   Yes, it does.

JOHN (*reasonably*)   Well now, look. There's a European war blowing up, there's a coal strike on, there's a fair chance of civil war in Ireland. . . . Surely you must see that it is a little out of proportion –

(*Pause. Catherine raises her head slowly.*)

CATHERINE (*with some spirit*)   All I know is, John, that if ever the time comes that the House of Commons has so much on its mind that it can't find time to discuss a Ronnie Winslow and his bally postal order, this country will be a far poorer place than it is now. (*Wearily.*) But you needn't go on, John dear. You've said quite enough. I entirely see your point of view.

(pp. 74–5)

Making this decision must have been a great struggle. By carrying on with the case, she loses John. She is almost thirty, and at the turn of the century there was a strong possibility that she would remain an old maid. Any decision of such major importance has a great influence on our future lives. We cannot be fully aware of the consequences until the decision has been followed through. This is part of the difficulties that face families each time a decision must be made. In the case of shared decisions this can be a little easier, in that there are a number of people all examining and evaluating difficulties and alternatives. Although this process is more intricate, the chances are that a better decision will be made.

At no time in this play does the whole family sit down and completely share the making of a decision. Rather there is a series of dyad decisions, which always involve the father on the one hand, and the person most intimately concerned on the other. The father has the role of the ultimate decision-maker, except in the case of the daughter. It is almost as if, at such times, the father is the family representative. This pattern probably fits very well in its historical context, and may even be enlightened.

However, today, with the emergence of the more democratic family structure, it is more likely that a 'shared' decision will be just that – shared by the whole family.

In a previous section we said that decisions have consequences. Sometimes a decision can precipitate a crisis.

Crisis

Each family has crises – but what constitutes a crisis may be different for each family. For example, the birth of a new baby may provoke a real crisis by placing too much extra strain on the emotional and economic resources of the family. On a different level, burglary of a household can precipitate an equally major crisis, despite whether the goods are insured or not. For some people, being robbed is almost like a violation of their own person.

There are no rules as to what may create a crisis for a family. In the Winslow family it is the father's sense of honour, and the belief that his son is telling the truth when he says he did not steal the money.

The crisis affects each individual family member in a different way. Often it is particularly difficult for the mother, for it is her role to support her husband whilst he is the man of action. Also she is the one who has most casual contact with the outside world – with the neighbours and shop-keepers, etc. At the same time she is expected to be loyal and loving. The strain of this role is very great, and sometimes she will need to lash out:

ARTHUR Facts are brutal things.
GRACE (*a shade hysterically*) Facts? I don't think I know what the facts are anymore –
ARTHUR The facts at this moment, are that we have a half of the income we had a year ago and we're living at nearly the same rate. However you look at it that's bad economics –
GRACE I'm not talking about economics, Arthur. I'm talking about ordinary common or garden facts – things we took for granted a year ago but which now don't seem to matter anymore.
ARTHUR Such as?

GRACE (*with rising voice*) Such as a happy home and peace and quiet and an ordinary respectable life, and some sort of future for us and our children. In the last year you've thrown all of that overboard, Arthur. There's your return for it, I suppose (*She indicates the headline in the newspaper*) and it's all very exciting and important, I'm sure, but it doesn't bring back any of the things that we've lost. I can only pray to God that you know what you're doing.

(*With sudden violence*) Oh, I wish I could see the sense of it all. You talk about sacrificing everything for him; but when he's grown up he won't thank you for it, Arthur – even though you have given your life to – publish his innocence as you call it.

(*Arthur makes an impatient gesture.*)

Yes, Arthur – your life. You talk gaily about arthritis and a touch of gout and old age and the rest of it, but you know as well as any of the doctors really what is the matter with you. (*Nearly in tears.*) You're destroying yourself, Arthur, and me and your family besides. For what, I'd like to know? I've asked you and Kate to tell me a hundred times – but you never will. For what, Arthur?

(*Arthur has struggled painfully out of his seat and now approaches her.*)

ARTHUR For Justice, Grace.

GRACE That sounds very noble. Are you sure it's true? Are you sure it isn't just plain pride and self-importance and sheer brute stubbornness?

ARTHUR (*putting a hand out*) No, Grace. I don't think it is. I really don't think it is –

GRACE (*shaking off his hand*) No. This time I'm not going to cry and say I'm sorry, and make it all up again. I can stand anything if there is a reason for it. But for no reason at all, it's unfair to ask so much of me. It's unfair –

(*She breaks down.*)

(pp. 63–4)

The Winslow family is able to handle its crisis. There is enough accompanying strains and pressures. Some families are unable to do this and may seek treatment. We have already discussed some factors which may contribute to such a situation. For example that of openly expressed love, secrets, confused communication, and perhaps a tendency to blame each other. A case history may illustrate this:

> This American family was seen at the request of their Pastor. The presenting problem was the sixteen-year-old daughter Susan, who had been caught shop-lifting. The rest of the family was comprised of a nineteen-year-old university student, mother who was a housewife and church-worker, and father who was an engineer. During the three months of sessions, meeting twice weekly, it developed that the mother and father (aged forty and forty-two respectively) had not had any sexual contact in 18 months. The young man was presented as a model son. He rarely communicated with the other members of the family. The family seldom did anything together, except to attend church every Sunday. This turned out to be an extremely private family, with each member spending as much time as possible in their own rooms. There was almost no conversation at the dinner table unless the family discussed the weather or the high cost of living.

> The sixteen-year-old daughter stole 200 dollars' worth of goods, none of which she kept. She gave it all away to her boy friends in an attempt to buy their friendships. She was a pretty girl, but not very popular. She had no idea of how to show her feelings. She came from a home where it was wrong to show any kind of feeling. In this family it was not possible to show pain with another member. The shoplifting was perceived by the therapist as a distress signal, as a cry for help.

> The role of the therapist was to act as a teacher, and the task was to open as many 'exits' as possible, thus allowing the family to express all kinds of feelings that had hitherto been suppressed. A second task was to teach the family how to express feelings in a non-verbal way. Once the family could see that nothing drastic happened as a result of openness, treatment was well on its way.

All crises bring with them suffering and pain. It is what the family does with this that dictates the nature of the experience. In a crisis, each family member must face himself, and re-evaluate the meaning of his relationships with others. In some families this may mean that the relationships must end – and this can be a kind of growth. In other families the pain and suffering may be transcended, and new ways found for expressing love and caring.

As an aside it is a legitimate question to ask 'What is a crisis?' The significance of an event is in the mind of the person who perceives it. It is he who defines it and imparts to it a significance. If we consider for example, a family who returns home to discover that their house is burning down. The family could respond in a number of ways. It could be a major tragedy, over which the family could become severely depressed. Or, philosophically, the family could immediately begin to consider the significance of this for their future lives. External factors, such as whether the house is insured or not, could possibly be very important here.

Following this line of reasoning, we may even encounter the family who actually manufactures crisis – for ulterior reasons. For such a family, such a crisis is highly functional, in that it may help them to avoid looking at their feelings, for example. Though of course when they meet the therapist, they will blame the crisis for whatever unhappiness they feel, and often present a façade of being highly motivated for change.

A crisis places great pressures on relationships. In ideal terms then, crisis should promote even better communications.

Communication

The style and content of communication within a family reveals to the trained observer the nature of the family, and tells us whether it is healthy or unhealthy.

There are many definitions of good communication. For our purposes we consider a number of dimensions. First, there should be a congruence between what is said and what is done, verbal and non-verbal statement should match. Second, there should be a willingness to listen very carefully to what others are saying. This means that we will not interrupt whilst others are talking, and will strive to understand the essence of what they are trying to say, and respond to that. Third, there will be in evidence a spontaneity and an honesty, which means that each individual has the means to express himself without fear. Fourth, there will be parity and commitment. The individual strives to make all his messages as clear as possible, so that there is no trace of ambiguity or confusion. This will involve him committing himself to thoughts and feelings quite openly and honestly.

There is also an element of competition in communication. Depending on how this is used, it can be destructive or it can be a learning experience. The modern debate can be a good example of this, where the competition inherent in the situation can spur the opposing individuals to greater heights of eloquence and thought. However, the other side of the coin is the danger that someone involved in the competition begins to perceive themselves as a failure – and this of course has quite the opposite effect in that it will depress and lead to the feeling that self is being devalued.

Communication in a crisis may often be very difficult. This is because each individual responds in his own way to the crisis, and in doing so emphasizes his difference. The communication can fall into a number of patterns.

One pattern might be to stop talking altogether. One such family consisted of mother, father and three children. At the time of treatment the parents had not been talking for six months. The only way they got messages to each other was through the children and through notes. During therapy it emerged that the reason the parents had stopped talking was because they were afraid. Whenever a crisis was precipitated, they responded by becoming angry. This was not acceptable to either parent – mother was afraid of possible physical violence, and the father afraid of losing face and being seen as a bad parent. Thus, after a while, the only way they could handle their feelings was simply to stop talking. This kind of silence can be deadly. It can burn the person inside and even eventually lead to a number of psychosomatic ailments.

There are a number of other, destructive ways in which families deal with crisis. Although, by and large, it tends to be a lower-class phenomenon, another way is to become physically violent. Yet other ways of meeting a crisis could be by scapegoating or falling sick. On the other hand, a healthy family will have very different strategies. No matter what class the family belongs to, humour, for example, is a universal phenomenon. The very existence of a humour in which everyone can share at a time of crisis presupposes certain conditions. Each family will tend to have its own style of humour, clearly understood by each member. This reduces to a minimum the chances of being misunderstood. It also allows for spontaneity. The Winslows display a sense of humour:

VIOLET   There was a bit in the *Evening News*. Did you read it, sir?

ARTHUR   No, what did it say?

VIOLET   Oh, about how it was a fuss about nothing and a shocking waste of the Government's time, but how it was a good thing all the same because it could only happen in England –

ARTHUR   There seems to be a certain lack of logic in that argument.

VIOLET   Well, perhaps they put it a bit different, sir. Still, that's what it said all right. And when you think it is all because of our Master Ronnie – I have to laugh about it sometimes, I really do. Wasting the Government's time at his age! I never did. Well, wonders will never cease.

ARTHUR   I know. Wonders will never cease.

VIOLET   Well – would that be all, sir?

ARTHUR   Yes, Violet. That will be all.

(*Catherine comes in.*)

CATHERINE   Good evening, Violet.

VIOLET   Good evening, Miss.

(*She goes out.*)

CATHERINE   Hullo, Father. (*She kisses him. Indicating Ronnie.*) An honourable Member described that this evening as a piteous little figure, crying aloud to humanity for justice and redress. I wish he could see him now.

ARTHUR   But what about *our* case? Is he going to allow us a fair trial?

CATHERINE   Apparently not.

ARTHUR   But that's iniquitous. I thought he would be forced to –

CATHERINE   I thought so, too. The House evidently thought otherwise.

ARTHUR   Will there be a division?

CATHERINE   There may be. If there is, the Government will win.

ARTHUR   What is the motion?

CATHERINE   To reduce the First Lord's salary by a hundred
pounds. (*With a faint smile.*) Naturally no one really wants
to do that.

(pp. 65–6)

Even at the height of the crisis, the eldest son can still joke – and
still be understood:

DICKIE   I had to fight my way in through an army of
reporters and people –

GRACE   Yes, I know. You didn't say anything, I hope, Dickie
dear. It's better not to say a word.

DICKIE   I don't think I said anything much . . . (*Carelessly.*)
Oh, yes, I did say that I personally thought he did it –

GRACE (*horrified*)   Dickie! You didn't.

(*He is smiling at her.*)
Oh, I see, it's a joke. You must not say things like that,
even in fun, Dickie dear –

DICKIE   How's it all going?

As we can see from this above quotation, humour can be used
to reduce tension and relieve feelings, and at the same time can
reinforce the existence of the close and trusting relationship.

Another potentially delicate issue is also dealt with in a humor-
ous way. This concerns Violet, the maid. A number of times the
Winslows have discussed whether or not she should be asked to
give notice, as the money is becoming so tight. During the trial
Dickie returns from Reading and seems a little surprised that
Violet is still there:

DICKIE   Is Violet still with you? She was under sentence last
time I saw you –

GRACE   She's been under sentence for the last six months,
poor thing – only she doesn't know it. Neither your father
nor I have the courage to tell her –

ARTHUR (*stopping at the door*)   I have the courage to tell her.

GRACE   It's funny that you don't, then, dear.

ARTHUR   I will.

GRACE (*hastily*)   No, no, you mustn't. When it's to be done,
I'll do it.

ARTHUR You see, Dickie, these taunts of cowardice are daily flung at my head; but should I take them up I'm forbidden to move in the matter. Such is the logic of women.

(pp. 81–2)

Handling difficult situations in a humorous way is one method, but sooner or later it is important to become serious. The healthy family will be able to communicate information about facts, thoughts and feelings, in a direct, open and honest fashion. To be able to communicate in this way without succumbing to stress reveals a high level of maturity. It also speaks volumes about the quality of the relationships which the family members enjoy. In a lengthy discussion between father and daughter, shortly after the daughter has been proposed to by an old admirer, a number of delicate subjects are touched upon – and all are dealt with calmly:

ARTHUR Oh. What did Desmond want?

CATHERINE To marry me.

ARTHUR I trust the folly you were referring to wasn't your acceptance of him?

CATHERINE (*smiling*) No, Father. (*She comes and sits on the arm of his chair.*) Would it be such folly, though?

ARTHUR Lunacy.

CATHERINE Oh, I don't know. He's nice, and he is doing very well as a solicitor.

ARTHUR Neither very compelling reasons for marrying him.

CATHERINE Seriously, I shall have to think it over.

ARTHUR Think it over, by all means. But decide against it.

CATHERINE I'm nearly thirty, you know.

ARTHUR Thirty isn't the end of life.

CATHERINE It might be – for an unmarried woman, with not much looks.

ARTHUR Rubbish.

(*Catherine shakes her head.*)

Better to live and die an old maid than marry Desmond.

CATHERINE Even an old maid must eat.

(*Pause.*)

ARTHUR I am leaving you and your mother everything, you know.

CATHERINE (*quietly*) Everything?

ARTHUR There is still a little left. . . .

CATHERINE   John's going to get married next month.

ARTHUR   Did he tell you?

CATHERINE   Yes. He was very apologetic.

ARTHUR   Apologetic!

CATHERINE   He didn't need to be. It's a girl I know slightly.
  She'll make him a very good wife.

ARTHUR   Poor Kate!
(*Pause. He takes her hand slowly.*)
  How I've messed up your life, haven't I.

CATHERINE   No, Father. Any messing up that's been done
  has been done by me.

ARTHUR   I'm so sorry, Kate. I'm so sorry.

CATHERINE   Don't be, Father. We both knew what we were
  doing.

ARTHUR   Did we?

CATHERINE   I think we did.

ARTHUR   Yet our motives seem to have been different all
  along – yours and mine, Kate? Can we both have been right?

CATHERINE   I believe we can. I believe we have been.

ARTHUR   And yet they've always been so infernally logical,
  our opponents, haven't they?

CATHERINE   I'm afraid logic has never been on our side. . . .
  If you could go back, Father, and choose again – would
  your choice be different?

ARTHUR   Perhaps.

CATHERINE   I don't think so.

ARTHUR   I don't think so, either.

CATHERINE   I still say we both knew what we were doing.
  And we were right to do it.

(*Arthur kisses the top of her head.*)

ARTHUR   Dear Kate. Thank you.

                                         (pp. 89–91)

Another important area when we are discussing communication, is how we express affection. It is difficult to generalize, as the
ways by which affection is expressed vary greatly, not only from
country to country, but between groups in the same country. For
example the difference between Italy and Sweden is very great;
in the latter general touching or embracing to demonstrate
affection is generally not practised, although this is now changing

a little amongst the younger generation, whereas in Italy flamboyant and public touching is the rule rather than the exception.

In England encounter and sensitivity training is a growing movement, reflecting, the authors feel, a growing awareness of the importance of touch, and a growing desire to express emotions through this means. But it can be difficult. For each time we reach out to touch someone we are taking a risk. The close and interdependent relationships that usually exist between family members generally make the business of touching much easier. However, the very importance of such relationships means that, in a crisis situation where we might be unsure of the other's response, reaching out to touch might seem a very hazardous venture. For example, if the husband and wife have quarrelled and have not settled their differences before returning to their bed, often one partner will attempt the reconciliation by reaching out to the other. There is always the possibility of total rejection, which is what increases the risk. (Fortunately the possible reward is equally great!)

The healthy family shares pain, the unhealthy family doesn't. Sharing is giving and receiving. Most people like to share happiness. For example, the winners of football pools usually like to share their miraculous good fortune with those people who matter to them. But few desire to share bad fortune. The man who has just been informed that he has terminal cancer is unlikely to shout his news from the roof tops. In the healthy family pain is shared more often than not, and serves the purpose of bringing people closer together. At the beginning the Winslow boy returns home from the Naval Training School. He has been expelled for stealing. He is ashamed and frightened. One by one he has to meet and face the members of his family. He is 14 years old. His first encounter is with his sister:

CATHERINE (*gently*) What's the trouble darling? You can tell me. . . . Have you run away?
(*Ronnie shakes his head, evidently not trusting himself to speak.*)
  What is it, then?
(*Ronnie pulls the document from his pocket which we have seen him reading in an earlier scene, and slowly hands it to her. Catherine reads it quietly.*)
  Oh, God!

RONNIE I didn't do it.

(*Catherine re-reads the letter in silence.*)

RONNIE Kate, I didn't. Really I didn't.

CATHERINE (*abstractedly*) No, darling. (*She seems uncertain as to what to do.*) This letter is addressed to Father. Did you open it?

RONNIE Yes.

CATHERINE You shouldn't have done that –

RONNIE I was going to tear it up. . . . Kate – shall we tear it up now?

CATHERINE No, darling.

RONNIE We could tell Father the term had ended two days sooner –

CATHERINE No, darling.

RONNIE I didn't do it – really I didn't –

(pp. 23–4)

This episode demonstrates how even in a healthy family, it is difficult to share pain and doubt openly at times. The news is shared with each member of the family in turn.

His second meeting is with his brother. It is interesting to contrast the way in which first Catherine and now Dickie respond to the news that Ronnie gives them:

DICKIE What's up, old chap?

RONNIE Nothing.

DICKIE Come on – tell me.

RONNIE It's all right.

DICKIE Have you been sacked?

(*Ronnie nods.*)

Bad luck. What for?

RONNIE (*in a low voice*) Stealing.

DICKIE (*evidently relieved*) Oh, is that all? Good Lord! I didn't know they sacked chaps for *that* in these days.

RONNIE I didn't do it.

DICKIE Why, good Heavens, at school we used to pinch everything we could jolly well lay our hands on.

(pp. 24–5)

At this point the mother arrives. She shows her concern in a very different way. She is very maternal and protective, rushing her son off with her, so that she can be alone with him and look after him. For the first time Ronnie is able to cry:

GRACE There, darling! It's all right, now.
(*Ronnie begins to cry quietly, his head buried in her dress.*)
RONNIE (*his voice muffled*) I didn't do it, mother.
GRACE No, darling. Of course you didn't. We'll go upstairs now, shall we, and get out of those nasty wet clothes.
RONNIE Don't tell Father.
GRACE No, darling. Not yet. I promise. Come along now.
(*She leads him towards the door held open by Catherine.*)
Your new uniform, too. What a shame.

(p. 25)

Now everyone knows except for the father. And now there begins what looks like a conspiracy to keep the news away from the father. We can only interpret the reason for this, but it would appear reasonable to assume two possible causes for this behaviour. First, they may believe Ronnie guilty of stealing (childish prank gone wrong), and second, that the father may assume a stern and authoritarian position towards his son. Violet lets the news slip out that Ronnie is home, and the father has to be informed of what has happened:

(*She goes out.*)
ARTHUR (*to Catherine*) Did *you* know Ronnie was back?
CATHERINE Yes –
ARTHUR And you, Dickie?
DICKIE Yes, father.
ARTHUR Grace?
GRACE (*helplessly*) We thought it best you shouldn't know – for the time being. Only for the time being, Arthur.
ARTHUR (*slowly*) Is the boy very ill?
(*No one answers. Arthur looks from one face to another in bewilderment.*)
Answer me, some one! Is the boy very ill? Why must I be kept in the dark like this? Surely I have the right to know. If he's ill I must be with him –
CATHERINE (*steadily*) No father. He's not ill.
(*Arthur suddenly realizes the truth from her tone of voice.*)
ARTHUR Will someone tell me what has happened, please?

29

(*Grace looks at Catherine with helpless inquiry. Catherine nods. Grace takes the letter from her dress.*)

GRACE   He brought this letter for you, Arthur.

(*She turns away quickly to hide her tears. Catherine puts a comforting arm on her shoulder. Arthur has not changed his attitude. There is a pause during which we can hear the sound of a gong in the hall outside.*)

ARTHUR (*at length*)   Desmond – be so good as to call Violet.

(*Desmond does so. There is another pause until Violet comes in.*)

VIOLET   Yes, sir.

ARTHUR   Violet, will you ask Master Ronnie to come down and see me, please?

GRACE   Arthur – he's in bed.

ARTHUR   You told me he wasn't ill.

GRACE   He's not at all well.

ARTHUR   Do as I say, please, Violet.

(pp. 31–2)

This episode demonstrates how, even in a healthy family, it is difficult to share pain and doubt openly at times. The rest of the family were afraid of what might happen between father and son. Their fears were not realized:

ARTHUR   Come in.

(*Ronnie appears in the doorway. He is in a dressing gown. He stands on the threshold.*)

    Come in and shut the door.

(*Ronnie closes the door behind him.*)

    Come over here.

(*Ronnie nods.*)

    Do you remember once, you promised me that if ever you were in trouble of any sort you'd come to me first?

RONNIE   Yes, Father.

ARTHUR   Why didn't you come to me now? Why did you have to go and hide in the garden?

RONNIE   I don't know, Father.

ARTHUR   Are you so frightened of me?

(*Ronnie does not reply. Arthur gazes at him for a moment then picks up the letter.*)

    In this letter it says you stole a postal order.

(*Ronnie opens his mouth to speak. Arthur stops him.*)

Now, I don't want you to say a word until you've heard
what I've got to say. If you did it, you must tell me. I
shan't be angry with you, Ronnie – provided you tell me
the truth. But if you tell me a lie I shall know it, because
a lie between you and me can't be hidden. I shall know it,
Ronnie – so remember that before you speak. (*Pause.*) Did
you steal this postal order?

RONNIE (*without hesitation*)   No, Father. I didn't.

(*Arthur continues to stare into his eyes for a moment then relaxes
and pushes him gently away.*)

ARTHUR   Go on back to bed.

(*Ronnie goes gratefully to the door.*)

And in future I trust that a son of mine will at least show
enough sense to come in out of the rain.

RONNIE   Yes, Father.

(pp. 33–4)

The Winslows tried to protect Ronnie because they were afraid
of the consequences of being open. Most people who refuse to
share their pain do so for similar reasons. We can call these 'the
myths of fear'. Let us examine a few of these myths. Probably the
most common is the fear of rejection. But what does this mean?
Most of us have suffered some sort of rejection. It is only by sharing the good and bad things that we discover the limits of our
relationships. The person who is rejected must then search for
alternatives, which search may help to make him stronger and
also to grow.

Another myth is that by sharing pain you are showing to the
other person your weakness, and by doing so we must make ourselves vulnerable, and open to further hurt. It is almost as if,
by sharing, we place ourselves in the other person's power – even
open to blackmail. But if we consider this for a moment, even
though it may feel to be true, it really is not a reality. It is true
that we become more vulnerable in the act of sharing, but if we
choose the recipients of our feelings carefully, and hence are able
to trust, the act of becoming vulnerable can be helpful rather than
hurtful, healing rather than damaging.

A third and final myth we shall discuss is the myth of misplaced
altrusim. This is where we rationalize our own refusal to share

31

pain on the grounds that we do not wish to make our families suffer what we are suffering. Hence we may bottle the feelings up inside ourselves, privately acting the martyr, believing that we are doing everyone a good turn. The cancer patient, already mentioned, who keeps his information to himself, might be an example. The only problem with this method is that by keeping our feelings or thoughts a secret we block whole areas of ourselves away from our families. It is almost as though we assume a secret existence inside of ourselves.

We have noted that a crisis places great pressure on relationships. It also places great pressure on the single individual, and thus might sometimes be reflected in his physical health.

Physical health in family life

The majority of people who go to see a doctor are suffering from some kind of psychosomatic ailment. By 'psychosomatic' we mean that the person's physical illness may have its origins in a psychological problem. The corollary of this is that if the psychological problem remains after the onset of the illness, and is tackled and understood by the patient, it is likely that the physical illness, too, will disappear.

An important study, *Sickness and Society* by Duff and Hollingshead, which looks at the family relationships of patients in a medical hospital states that (1968, p. 248):

> After examining systematically all the data on each family,
> we made an assessment of evidence on the contribution of the
> patients' involvement in family relationships to the
> development of the illness. We found that 40 per cent of the
> patients' illnesses were linked definitely into the family
> relationships, and 53 per cent were not.

A dramatic example was demonstrated by a family who came to treatment:

> The 16-year-old son who was in a residential unit for
> delinquent boys suffered heavily from an incurable psoriasis.
> The rest of the family consisted of a 42-year-old step-father
> who was a doctor and a 38-year-old mother who was a

housewife. The mother was unusually attractive, and it quickly became obvious in the course of therapy that there were strong sexual feelings between mother and son. It soon became apparent that this unspoken incest, completely unnoticed by the father, was at the root of the family problem. Gradually the painful area was broached, and amazingly, shortly after it was shared by the whole family, the boy's psoriasis completely disappeared. For a while, everything seemed well. After a few weeks, on week-end leave, the boy had a major argument with his mother. Upon return to the unit it was noticed that the disease had flared up once more. The problems were once again discussed and brought out into the open, and again the trouble disappeared. The length of the treatment was four months. At the end of that time the relationships within the family seemed much more stable. Just as important, the boy had learned that, for him at least, openness and clarity were vital in his relationships if he were to maintain his health.

Illness may be generated by emotional disturbance, but equally well, existing illness can be aggravated by the onset of further disturbance. Mr Arthur Winslow, in just about two years, is reduced from simply using a cane for support to having to be wheeled around in a bath chair, his health has deteriorated so much. His health is so bad, that by the time the trial has come to a climax, his family is discussing it in very, very gloomy terms:

DICKIE (*seriously*) How *is* he?
(*Grace shakes her head quietly.*)
   Will you take him away after the trial?
GRACE 'He's promised to go into a nursing home.
DICKIE Do you think he will?
GRACE How do I know? He'll probably find some new excuse –
DICKIE But surely, if he loses this time, he's lost for good, hasn't he?
GRACE (*slowly*) So they say, Dickie dear – I can only hope that it's true.
DICKIE How did you keep him away from the trial?
GRACE Kate and Sir Robert together. He wouldn't listen to me or the doctor.

(p. 82)

33

The strain that was placed upon the Winslow family, beginning with Mr Winslow's decision to fight the Admiralty, must have been enormous. In the course of two years the family name was to become almost a byword in England. Not only for their courage and determination, but also for what must have seemed to many people their stupidity. They gambled most of the family fortune. The daughter felt forced to break off her engagement. The eldest son had to leave college. And all this for the sake of a young boy who probably didn't realize what all the fuss was about most of the time. The impact of all this tension must have contributed to the worsening of Arthur Winslow's health, particularly since he was the head of the family and most responsible for what happened. The interplay between emotion and physical well-being has always been well known. Yet science in its denial of philosophy has tended to minimize and even ignore this relationship. A. R. K. Mitchell says in his book *Psychological Medicine in Family Practice* (1971, p. 117):

> 'For this is the greatest error of the day that the physicians separate the soul from the body.' Plato was talking of the medical philosophy of his day, and such criticism can be levelled at ourselves, for we still labour under the cross of Cartesian Dualism. . . . We know or ought to know, that man is an entity of body and mind. These two components are only ways of thinking about ourselves. The split between them does not exist in reality but only in our thinking. Thomas Szasz has warned us that it is a common human error to think that a thing exists, even, if necessary inventing it, and then to act as if it had reality and it was not just part of our conceptual thinking. Body and mind are not separate but part of each other, different aspects of the same whole.

Particularly since the Second World War, psychosomatic medicine has increased, although it is still only a small part of the field of medicine. The whole area of psychosomatic medicine is controversial. A major part of the controversy is our ignorance, our lack of knowledge. If we return to Mitchell for a moment, he describes the limits of our present knowledge (1971):

Thus the following can be classed as defined psychosomatic disorders – migraine, hypertension, hyperthyroidism, allergic rhinitis, hay fever, asthma, peptic ulcer, colitis, impotence, frigidity, and certain forms of dermatitis. Some would also include cases of diabetes mellitus. Unfortunate misunderstanding can still arise and asthma provides us with a good example. Asthma is classed as one of the psychosomatic disorders and some people think that this is an all exclusive statement. In other words, that all cases of asthma are psychosomatic. This could be true but is not proven. What is really meant is that some cases of asthma are psychosomatic. We are back again to the idea of a spectrum. At one end there are cases in which asthma is due to damage in the bronchii from allergic or infective processes, and at the other end there are cases in which psychological factors predominate. In the middle there are cases where organic and psychological factors are equally represented. It is those cases where attacks of asthma appear to be triggered-off and run parallel to crisis and emotional stress that should properly be called psychosomatic. In contrast, those attacks which serve clearly defined psychological needs should be called psychogenic asthma.

If we think of illness as an event, it will have certain consequences for tight-knit families. Schedules will have to be altered, roles will be re-defined (for example, children may have to become domestically responsible whereas before they might not have been); feelings will have to be re-evaluated; sacrifices may have to be made and other things too might have to change. For the patient there is usually a sharply defined role change; and there are a number of secondary compensations. These may include less responsibility, more affection and attention, and often involves the patient being protected from anything which may possibly disturb or upset him. A number of writers have described models by which people may become either criminal or mentally ill.[1] These models describe a process by which a person can achieve such statuses. It is also possible to think in similar terms regarding the process of becoming medically sick. Normally people do not get sick by accident – they must prepare for it. We suggest that, as part of this 'preparation', the person experiences a series of prior events each of which contributes a little more to the tensions and pressures he feels. We further submit that eventually sickness is the way the person deals with these pressures, in that before he had not faced the problem satisfactorily. In this way sickness can be seen as a cry for help, and this is that the person can no longer cope on his own with his situation.

It is in this case that the therapist must be sensitive to the needs of his client, for there is always the possibility of genuine organic damage. In which case of course the client needs to be sent to a medical doctor. If there is no organic damage, then he simply treats the physical symptoms as part of the pathology. At times the therapist must be aware that the clients will often suffer intense pain as the real problems are approached and uncovered. A client may suddenly become sick, or a physical illness may be increased. The therapist must be prepared to deal with both possibilities.

Thinking within this frame of reference, the role of the medical doctor assumes a new significance. Whether he admits it or not, he has to assume at least partially the role of therapist. He handles the symptoms of loneliness, despair and frustration every day. In fact he is presented with an unrivalled opportunity to do a great deal of preventive work. This might be the ideal, but the fact remains that it does not happen. The medical practitioner today is not recognized by his clients as a therapist – they insist upon placing their problems within a medical framework, thus placing the doctor in an ambiguous position. On the one hand he must offer some medical explanation for the illness, and on the other often he will be thinking in purely psychological terms as to the origin of the illness.

The open family system

Is it possible for a person to be completely free whilst he is living with others? This is a question which has been debated by philosophers for many centuries. The exponents of the opposing camps, some believing that man could be free, others that it was impossible, found their champions in the philosophers Mill and Hobbes. Mill, as particularly found in his essay *On Liberty*, believed in freedom, basing his philosophy on the assumption that man's nature was basically good and benevolent, and that it was only the corrupting influences of society which made him otherwise. Hobbes (see his work *Leviathan*), on the other hand, believed that life was nasty, brutish and short. He believed that, if unchecked, society would be a war of all against all, and that it was only social control which prevented such anarchy from emerging.

These beliefs were carried over to the twentieth-century discipline of psychology. On the one hand humanistic psychology – epitomized by the young Carl Rogers – believed that in our society man somehow became estranged from his true self. This means that, to Rogers, man was perceived in Millian terms as being basically good. Freud, though, was clear and adamant, but in the opposite direction. The libido, unless checked by moral and social rules, was a rapacious non-caring drive, and unless they were carefully checked, such drives were potentially destructive, both for the self and others.

For many years now there has been in wide circulation the myth of the permissive society – a society where particularly the young have the freedom to express themselves in any way they wish. We know that this is not true, and that simply there have been some changes in moral attitude, particularly regarding sex, although investigation reveals that even these changes are not all-pervasive. Equally there has developed the myth, apparently supported by some psychological theory, that the 'good family' is the one where everyone, particularly the children, are free to do just what they want.

What are the implications for a family which tries to be totally free? It means that no thought, action, or feeling, or any event which affects directly or indirectly any member of the family can be secret or private. It also means that no one person can impose their desires or will on any other person. If we think for a moment about the practical implications of this we might be a little surprised. For example, preferably it would mean no doors – either on the bedroom or the bathroom, our two sacred rooms. Lovemaking and going to the toilet cease to be private and personal and become public affairs. This of course might pose problems for our friends, neighbours and relatives. Further difficulties would be encountered by the family who wish to follow a nudist philosophy in their own homes.

In our fantasy family, openness is one issue and the other major issue is control. What do family members do in the face of another member's difficult behaviour. How would we cope with open genital play between a 5- and 7-year-old brother and sister? Would we have the tolerance of Maria, the mother of 'the children on the hill'? She responded in what was a very unusual way when her children showed a desire to play with their faeces (Deakin, 1972):

> Nor is she squeamish about excreta or other bodily functions, or nervously hyper-cautious about potentially damaging elements in the immediate environment. When the children decided to play 'potty bombs' she allowed this as she had allowed all of their exploratory play. For an afternoon they played messily in the bathroom. When their curiosity was slaked and the taboo seemed expurgated she cleaned up, and after this experience the children never wished to repeat the game or even referred to it. It needed considerable strength of conviction, but the effect justified overcoming what in effect might seem to be the adults' rather than the children's excretion taboo.

What do we do when the children petulantly refuse to go to school or start to destroy property? One of the authors encountered an interesting example of the possible complications involved in attempting to be totally free with child. During a family visit a young child, age six, proceeded to destroy two valuable original paintings. The host became visibly upset as the child proceeded to destroy the paintings which were hung on the wall. The host did not interfere because he felt that he had no right to interfere with someone else's child, besides which the child's father was also present. The paintings were completely destroyed. The host later sent his friend a bill for the cost of the paintings. The friend refused to meet any of the cost whatsoever. A close relationship came to an end. The father's rationale for not stopping the child was that he believed the child should be totally free, and not have any limits placed on him.

A. S. Neill is famous for his permissive atmosphere at Summerhill. Yet he himself is the first to point out that even the freedom his pupils enjoy is bounded by limits. Neill is speaking on childrearing and his ideas of self-regulation by the child (1968, pp. 104–5):

Self-regulation means the right of a baby to live freely,
without outside authority and things psychic and somatic.
It means that the baby feeds when it is hungry; that it
becomes clean in habits only when it wants to; that it is never
stormed at nor spanked; that it is always loved and protected.

It all sounds easy and natural and fine yet it is astounding
how many young parents, keen on the idea, manage to
misunderstand it. Tommy, age 4, bangs the notes of a
neighbour's piano with a wooden mallet. His fond parents
look on with a triumphant smile which means, 'Isn't self-
regulation wonderful? . . . Only a fool in charge of young
children would allow unbarred bedroom windows or an
unprotected fireplace in the nurseries. Yet, too often, young
enthusiasts for self-regulation come to my school as visitors,
and exclaim at our lack of freedom in locking poison in a lab.
closet, or our prohibition about playing on the fire escape.
The whole freedom movement is marred and despised because
so many advocates of freedom have not got their feet on the
ground.

One such protested to me recently because I had shouted
sternly at a problem boy of 7 who was kicking my office door.
His idea was that I should smile and tolerate the noise until
the child should live out his desire to bang doors. It is true
that I spent a good few years of my life patiently tolerating
the destructive behaviour of problem children, but I did this
as their psychological doctor and not as their fellow citizen.

If a young mother thinks her child of three should be
allowed to paint the front door with red ink on the ground
that he is thereby expressing himself freely, she is incapable
of grasping what self-regulation means.

I remember sitting with a friend at Covent Garden. During
the first ballet, a child in front of us talked loudly to her
father. At the end of the ballet, I found other seats. My
companion said to me 'What would you do if one of your
kids from Summerhill did that?' 'Tell him to shut up,' I
said.

Dr Haim G. Ginott, Professor of Psychology at the New York
University, makes an equally clear statement about limit-setting
(1970, p. 75):

It is preferable that a limit be total rather than partial. There is a clear distinction for example between not splashing water and not splashing water on sister. A limit that states, 'You may splash her a little, as long as you do not wet her too much,' is inviting a deluge of troubles. Such a vague statement leaves the child without a clear criterion for making decisions.

A limit must be stated firmly, so that it carries only one message to the child: 'This prohibition is definite. I mean business.' When a parent is not sure of what to do, it is best that he do nothing but think and clarify his own attitude. In setting limits, he who hesitates is lost in endless arguments. Restrictions, invoked haltingly and clumsily, become a challenge to children and evoke a battle of wills, which no one can win. A limit must be stated in a manner that is deliberately calculated to minimize resentment, and to save self esteem. The very process of limit setting should convey authority, not insults. It should deal with a specific event, not with a developmental history. Temptations to clean away all problems with one big sweep should be resisted.

Every individual is faced with the dilemma of control – to what extent should he impose his values on others? This is particularly true in close relationships, such as those which exist in close-knit families. An integral part of this dilemma is that, whether one wants to or not, we are bound to communicate something of our values and hence influence others. 'It is impossible not to communicate.' (See Watzlawick, Beavin and Jackson, 1968, pp. 48–51, 73–80.)

If we accept that inevitably our lives are bound to impinge on others, that we cannot avoid influencing others, that it is impossible to live in close contact with others and not establish some kind of limits, then the nature of the problem changes. The question we are now faced with is 'What kind of control?' All relationships are regulated by a series of spoken and unspoken rules, which usually can be changed by mutual agreements. The process of regulating relationships can be quite a complicated process in a family system because of the interdependent nature of the relationships. There are three possible categories of agreement: between parent and child; between child and parent; between child and child. Each of them can have their own peculiar difficulties. At first sight it may seem that agreement could be most easily reached between the parents, but this is not necessarily so. The conditions which govern the relationships and thus affect the agreements are different in each case. Parents can always escape, whereas until the child reaches a certain age escape for him is virtually impossible. The elder child may be physically bigger, and age and experience may allow him to bully his younger brothers and sisters. Parental intervention may be necessary before agreement can be reached.

The difficulties we have mentioned can be viewed in a different light. The family, by its nature, is exacting and demanding, but at the same time it provides a base from which it is possible to do almost anything. For many people the family provides a vehicle for exciting adventure. For example, many families set out on physical adventure such as sailing around the world for three years. Maria, with her children on the hill, embarked on an intellectual adventure, trying to find out if a particular kind of family could be translated into reality. She and her husband set out to create an environment in which the potential of their children could be fully and freely explored. This meant for them that they would have to devote fifteen years of their life as parents to the project. However, the family can also provide a third type of project. A few years ago in England there was published *The World of Nigel Hunt*, a remarkable diary written by a Mongol child (Hunt, 1967). His father was a headmaster and author. After the child's death the father stated that the birth of such a child was possibly the best thing that had ever happened to him, he had learned so much about life and himself. Such emotional adventure is possible to most family members. It is possible for everyone to grow.

We shall now explore the open family along three of its dimensions. Risk-taking and valuing are almost inseparable. People who are afraid to take risks are like that because they are afraid of the consequences. If a person notices that he is valued by the other family members – and he values them – then he will feel free to risk his feelings, confident that he will deal with the outcome. It is fairly common for the young adolescent to feel that it is impossible to openly express his feelings – either of love or hate – towards his parents. Adolescence is a time of inner turmoil, ideally just the time when we do need to communicate most of all. But somehow most young adults have learned that one does not speak of one's feelings, that one copes with them in other ways. Such learning must have taken place from the parents or even the grandparents. In the open family the children have been brought up to show respect for each other by being willing to share their feelings.

What is failure? What does it mean in an open family system when one fails to achieve what one has set out to do? One important thing is that when the child or the adult fails to achieve a predefined target, there is no shame involved or no blame directed at him. Instead efforts will be made to deal with the episode constructively, to see what can be learned from the experience to be applied in the future. In this way, so called 'failure' experiences are translated into rich sources of learning, and present failure can be used to lay out the foundation for future success. Examples are numerous of children who made what looked apparently like failure moves, who later went on to become great successes – people like Edison, Einstein, Bell, etc. If we measure success in terms of the individual's feelings of self-fulfilment, then it is important that we allow people to follow their own pathways. The high level of maturity in the Winslow family, for example, allowed father and eldest son to appraise Dickie's progress at university, and to reach an agreement that he was failing there and thus wasting the family's money. The relationship was not adversely affected by this decision, and a constructive alternative was found which allowed Dickie to maintain his self-respect and also that of his father.

Within the open family setting, and intimately related to what we have been discussing, is the idea of self-esteem and of how it is generated, and then maintained. To have high self-esteem we have to like ourselves, have a realistic image of who we are, and of our capabilities. How does this come about? At first, the image we have of ourselves is learned through our relationships with the rest of the family. Later this image can be changed or modified by other important relationships. To simply believe that we are pretty valuable people is, however, not enough. By interacting with others we are able to have an on-going assessment of ourselves through feed-back. Thus the most vital factor in building and maintaining self-esteem is clear and honest communication. As we shall see, in the Loman family, Willie attempts to maintain a false self-esteem based on fantasies. The rest of the family collude with this, with the result that Willie commits suicide. By contrast, in the Winslow family, we have seen a number of very different issues tackled in a very honest and direct fashion, with the result that no one's self-esteem was damaged.

The better the mental health of a family, the higher the self-esteem of its individual members. Thus, in one sense, we can say that the task of the therapist is to raise the self-esteem of the families. In order to do this it is crucial that he also must value himself highly. He must believe in himself, in what he is doing, and in his skills as a teacher.

The Synge family: *Riders to the Sea* by John Millington Synge

List of characters

Maurya	An old woman
Bartley	Her son
Cathleen	Her daughter
Nora	A younger daughter
The men and women	

Synopsis of the plot of the play

Michael, Cathleen and Nora's brother, has been missing for nine days. A bundle of clothes has been recovered along the coast – they were found on a body washed from the sea and it is possible that they may belong to Michael. They do. And within minutes of this realization they have brought the news that Bartley too is dead. For this family he is the eighth man to have died in the sea.

A death in the family

This play is set on an island off the west coast of Ireland at the turn of the century. The work of the men is fishing. At this time fishing was still a very dangerous occupation, and many men died. Fishing was the economic mainstay of the island, the basic means of survival. The only alternative would have been to have left the island.

43

The ruthless and dangerous occupation of fishing meant that death was a constant factor. The people adapted to this by creating a special culture. There is a kind of stoic acceptance of the inevitability of death. In this kind of community the person who mourns too openly, or voices their fears too loud, is the deviant.

The Synge play is a vignette, concentrating on the responses of the womenfolk to the deaths of the men in their families. In the play the women come to terms with the death of the two brothers within days of each other. This is a reality which we must all come to terms with at some time or other. The Synge family have one way of dealing with it, there are many others.

Our whole discussion of the Synge family revolves round death and survival.

Death and Survival

In the West we are trying to hide from death. More and more we are separating the old from the young. For example in Sweden and the USA, because the old are in special retirement homes and communities, the young rarely see death. In Sweden they are becoming aware of this as a problem, and one way they try to handle it is to get the young children to visit old folks' homes.

In hiding from death it becomes more and more of a taboo. We try to avoid the old, the infirm, the dying, by physically removing ourselves from them. Not only that, but we continue this denial by refusing to accept the reality of death itself. We do this in a number of ways: by elaborate funeral arrangements, by magnificent tombs, by elaborate release of rituals. Evelyn Waugh's famous parody *The Loved One*, based on an American cemetery and crematorium, is an example. Here the dead are beautified, the living comforted, and death becomes an illusion.

But does death have to be such a tragedy? Death, like sickness, can be seen as an event in the family. And, like an event, it will have certain consequences. Pain must be handled. It might mean, for example, re-negotiation with self and others, and certain practical consequences, which might include loss of status, different income, geographical movement, etc. Thus the event of death has two kinds of consequences, the emotional and the practical. Both have to be dealt with.

A case in point concerns the Lottso family. The wife fell seriously ill with cancer, and was hospitalized for a long time. The case was terminal. This was in America where treatment in hospital has to be paid for in some way by the individual. First of all, the medical insurance was exhausted. To help pay the cost, Mr Lottso sold his six-room family house, and moved with his grown-up children into a flat in a four-family house. The burden fell almost entirely onto Mr Lottso as the two sons were too busy to become involved. Within a year of Mrs Lottso's death, the husband was entirely on his own – his two sons had left; one had gone into the Army, the other had married and gone to another city (Duff and Hollingshead, 1968, p. 336):

> Depressed and isolated Mr Lottso was alone with his memories. . . . He said 'I wanted the best for her. I can honestly say I tried to give her the best of care, the best of doctors, the best of everything within my means, and even beyond my means. And if I had to do the same thing over again, which I hope to God I never have to, I wouldn't have done it any differently. My conscience is clear. I tried to give her the best.'

Mr Lottso is now on his own. Where does he go from here? Basically, he can do one of two things: he can remain as he is this moment, alone and isolated, or he can begin to think in terms of himself and his own future, and move out into a new life.

The woman's role in our society is generally different from that of a man. This will be reflected in the way she responds to death and dying. Her role can take a number of forms. It may be particularly difficult for her if it is the husband who dies. If she has children she will have to combine the roles of both mother and father. There is the further issue of outside relationships: once again she is alone and will probably begin thinking of relationships with men. (This may prove to be problematic if there are any children.) There are often the issues of money and work.

One particular type of woman's role is described in the Synge play. In this community they live with death. When the play opens the two sisters are in the kitchen. Nora has a package:

CATHLEEN (*spinning the wheel rapidly*) What is it you have?

NORA The young priest is after bringing them. It's a shirt and a plain stocking were got off a drowned man in Donegal.

(*Cathleen stops her wheel with a sudden movement and leans out to listen.*)

NORA We're to find out if it's Michael's they are, some time herself will be down looking by the sea.

CATHLEEN How would they be Michael's, Nora? How would he go the length of that way to the far north?

NORA The young priest says he's known the like of it. 'If it's Michael's they are,' says he, 'you can tell herself he's got a clean burial, by the grace of God; and if they're not his, let no one say a word about them, for she'll be getting her death,' says he, 'with crying and lamenting.'

(p. 19)

The Michael they are referring to is their brother. The important factor to notice in this brief extract is their calmness, efficiency and acceptance. There is no hysteria or denial; there is only the realization that they must check out the clothes to see if they really are Michael's, and the desire to keep their mother from needless suffering. They've had lots of practice. Seven members of their family, all the men except Bartley, have died. Maurya says:

I've had a husband, and a husband's father, and six sons in this house – six fine men, though it was a hard birth I had with every one of them and they coming into the world – and some of them were found and some of them were not found, but they're gone now, the lot of them. . . .

(p. 27)

The girls debate whether to examine the bundle now. They decide against it:

NORA Shall I open it now?

CATHLEEN Maybe she'd wake up on us and come in before we'd done. (*Coming to the table.*) It's a long time we'll be, and the two of us crying.

NORA (*goes to the inner door and listens*) She's moving about on the bed. She'll be coming in a minute.

CATHLEEN   Give me the ladder, and I'll put them up in the
loft, the way she won't know of them at all, and maybe
when the tide turns she'll be going down to see would he
be floating from the east.

(p. 20)

In the girls' desire to protect their mother, what is amazing is
their self-control. Cathleen's remark 'It's a long time we'll be, and
the two of us crying' reveals the whole different world. She knows
that she will mourn if the clothes really are Michael's, but here is
not the right time. The realities of life have to go on. When the
mother's grief feelings interfere with the practical issues of life,
her children are quite short with her:

BARTLEY (*getting his purse and tobacco*)   I'll have half an hour
to go down, and you'll see me coming again in two days,
or three days, or maybe in four days if the wind is bad.

MAURYA (*turning round to the fire, and putting her shawl over
her head*) Isn't it a hard and cruel man who won't hear a
word from an old woman, and she holding him from the
sea?

CATHLEEN   It's the life of a young man to be going on the sea,
and who would listen to an old woman with one thing and
she saying it over?

BARTLEY (*taking the halter*)   I must go now quickly. I'll ride
down on the red mare, and the grey pony'll run behind
me. . . . The blessing of God on you.

(*He goes out.*)

MAURYA (*crying out as he is in the door*)   He's gone now, God
spare us, and we'll not see him again. . . .

CATHLEEN   Why wouldn't you give him your blessing and he
looking round in the door?

(p. 22)

Grief obviously has its place, and Maurya's was inappropriate.
The young man makes his choice: it is dangerous but it is his
choice, and he demands that his family respect it. This is a
beautiful example high-lighting the idea of responsibility and
differentness. The son is his own master, he is in charge of his
own life. His chosen path brings with it the very real possibility
of death. He is about to go to sea with the horses on a day when

47

the sea is very rough and possibly dangerous. He assesses the risks and possible gains, and decides to go. Having made that decision the women-folk have no right whatsoever to interfere. He must be allowed to be different, and be responsible for his own decisions. Today this kind of choice is still made – if we think for a minute about the plight of coal miners with the unpleasant danger of mine collapse (as well as the perpetual threat to health) or of today's deep-sea fishermen. Racing driving is another, perhaps more dramatic, example where there is the continual prospect of serious injury or death.

In the Synge family when the prospect of death becomes real, they have their own way of dealing with it. First Maurya is told of Michael's death after the clothes have been checked, and within seconds she is told that Bartley, too, has died:

NORA They're carrying a thing among them, and there's water dripping out of it and leaving a track by the big stones.
CATHLEEN (*in a whisper to the women who have come in*) Is it Bartley it is?
ONE WOMAN It is, surely, God rest his soul.

MAURYA (*raising her head and speaking as if she did not see the people around her*) They're all gone now, and there isn't anything more the sea can do to me. . . . I'll have no call now to be up crying and praying when the wind breaks from the south, and you can hear the surf is in the east. . . . It's a great rest I'll have now, and great sleeping in the long nights after Samhain, if it's only a bit of wet flour we do have to eat, and maybe a fish that would be stinking. (*She kneels down again, crossing herself, and saying prayers under her breath.*)
CATHLEEN (*to an old man*) Maybe yourself and Eamon would make a coffin when the sun rises. We have fine white boards herself bought, God help her, thinking Michael would be found, and I have a new cake you can eat while you'll be working.

(pp. 28–9)

Maurya's days of tragedy are over. There are no more men left in the family. So suddenly she becomes calm and efficient, her grief controlled. There is the coffin to be made. At last Maurya has found a kind of peace:

> MAURYA (*puts the empty cup mouth downwards on the table, and lays her hands together on Bartley's feet*) They're all together this time, and the end has come. May the Almighty God have mercy on Bartley's soul, and on Michael's soul, and on the souls of Sheamus and Patch, and Stephen and Shawn (*bending her head*) and may He have mercy on my soul, Nora, and on the soul of every one is left living in the world.
>
> (*She pauses, and the keen rises a little more loudly from the women, then sinks away.*)
>
> MAURYA (*continuing*) Michael has a clean burial in the far north, by the grace of the Almighty God. Bartley will have a fine coffin out of the white boards, and a deep grave surely. What more can we want than that? No man at all can be living for ever, and we must be satisfied.

(p. 30)

However, the Synge family belong to a very special culture. Not everyone has the equanimity in the face of death that they do. In our society how do we deal with the prospect of the death of a family member?

We cannot make any sweeping statements. One obvious variable that will affect the way death is handled will be the size of the community. For example, in a very small village, where everyone knows everyone else, it is hardly likely that someone's terminal illness could or would be kept a secret. However, in the anonymity of the large city the degree of secrecy is liable to be highly marked.

Death, like life, is a process with a number of clearly defined stages. The first stage is the onset of an illness which is usually told to the family. A doctor – often a GP – will be consulted. The GP may send the patient to hospital if he believes the case to be serious enough. There it may be discovered that the patient has what is possibly a terminal illness. Treatment will be prescribed, usually involving a stay in the hospital. Every effort will be made to save the patient. However, if the doctors feel that no matter what they do the patient will not be saved, at some point they will cease curative treatment, and will be content with merely making the patient comfortable whilst waiting for him to die. The first serious decision-point in this process occurs when the doctors discover the patient is going to die. They will have to decide what they should tell, and to whom they should tell it. Many doctors refuse categorically to tell the patient: Duff and Hollingshead (1968, p. 310) quote that 25 per cent of doctors refused to tell their heart disease patients that they were dying but a massive total of 75 per cent refused to tell their cancer patients. Sometimes physicians avoid the real issue by telling only the family that the patient is dying. This can of course face the family with a very difficult moral and emotional problem – should they tell the patient, or should they not tell him in the hope that he will suffer less?

In 73% of the 37 expected deaths, a mutual decision was made by the physician and the family to avoid letting the sick person know the truth about his condition and its expected outcome. In 36% of these cases, the physician was instructed by the spouse or other family members *not* to disclose the truth to the patient. If the physician or the spouse believed that the 'patient should be protected' from the diagnosis and prognosis of his illness, elaborate stratagems were created to see that the sick person was deceived.

In a fairly new and very controversial book *On Death and Dying* (1970) Elisabeth Kubler-Ross talks of the same issue (p. 149):

Greatly dependent on the patient's attitude, awareness, and ability to communicate, the family then undergoes certain changes. If they are able to share their common concerns, they can take care of important matters early and under less pressure of time and emotion. If each one tries to keep a secret from the other, they will keep an artificial barrier between them which will make it difficult for any preparatory grief for the patient or his family. The end result will be much more dramatic than for those who can talk and cry together at times.

Here Dr Ross is advocating the idea of the open family as the best means of dealing with pain and suffering. No secrets, with the emphasis on sharing what is happening to each member no matter how difficult or painful it may be.

In the hospital where one might think that the idea of death is a familiar and accepted one, we find that the medical staff behave in strange ways. Duff and Hollingshead present us with an interview with a physician (1968, p. 316):

> He would lie there in his extremely wasted state, vomiting faeces, and with a keen eye to stare at me and ask if I thought he would die that day. It was terribly disconcerting, but not one of us had the guts to tell him that he was dying. He had 5 chemotherapy treatments for cancer and had some diarrhoea and some rather severe stomatitis which was extremely uncomfortable. He was a stalwart individual and extremely grateful for everything we could do for him, but it was difficult to say whether he thought we were just really doing something for him or that we were just a bunch of bastards.

Another report, this time from a paper presented to the World College of Nursing, the British Medical Association Conference, 'Partners in Patient Care' (London, 26 November 1971) by B. J. McNulty states that:

> Death is therefore looked upon as a failure to cure. The dying patient is, in a sense, an embarrassment. Where the staff is short, it is the patient with a good chance of recovery who absorbs much of the staff's attention. A dying patient will sometimes apologize for being such a trouble, even guilty perhaps for taking time from others. He is the exception and his uniqueness isolates him. For convenience the dying patient may be moved to a corner or a side ward and is thereby isolated even more. The breathless speed of a busy ward is ill-suited to the dying patient's need for tranquillity and peace.

People are not immortal, so why do so many hospital staffs try to pretend they are? What are the doctors and nurses frightened of? What is the worst that can happen if they are open and honest? Surely the very worst that could possibly happen is that the patient might die a little while sooner. The converse of this is that the patient can be given all the support that he may need to work through his emotions. It would cut out all the secrecy and fantasy that the patient is going to get well. It would simplify communication between the patient, family and physician. We

51

will suggest that the ways in which the medical staff behave is related to them attempting to take care of their own feelings rather than from any concern for the patient.

Possibly one of the reasons for this is the result of pressure the doctors receive from the patient's relatives and family (Duff and Hollingshead, 1968, p. 318):

> Patients and spouses expected physicians to offer treatment in the hope that the ravages of the disease would soon be stopped. This expectation was pressed upon the doctor so vigorously that, when possible they offered and even when a patient was dying, they offered the image of hope. In so doing almost all doctors discounted the severity of the disease and the grim prognosis while they proceeded to apply therapies which they knew were of little value. The importance of treatment was inflated beyond its true worth (this knowledge was rarely shared with the patient), while the realistic concerns of the family and its dying member were set aside and sometimes ignored. One physician told us: 'It gets sticky, sometimes awfully messy. You have to lie because there is no other way.' Another said 'This whole institution [the hospital] treats diseases, not people. I don't know really what we are achieving. Sometimes I think we ought to quit on some of these patients, but even to mention this raises eyebrows around here and people ask you, "What, aren't you going to operate on this cancer?" Others say "You aren't even going to take a look at it?" or, "What kind of doctor are you and what kind of hospital is this?"'

When it is known definitely that the patient has reached the terminal stage, a new actor may be called in. The clergyman may play a very important part for some people during illness or death. In *Riders to the Sea*, the priest, though never seen, is referred to many times. The Irish Catholic tradition is a very powerful one, and all the more so in a small close-knit community where death is continually present. However, religion no longer plays a central role in the lives of most people (Kubler-Ross, 1970, p. 13):

> What role has religion played in these changing times? In the old days more people seemed to believe in God

unquestionably; they believed in a hereafter, which was to relieve people of their suffering and pain. There was a reward in Heaven, and if we had suffered much here on earth we could be rewarded after death depending on the courage and grace, patience and dignity with which we had carried our burden. Suffering was more common, as child birth was natural and a long and painful event – but the mother was awake when the child was born. There was purpose and a future reward in suffering. Now we sedate mothers, try to avoid pain and agony; we may even induce labor to have a birth occur on a relative's birthday or to avoid interference with another important event. Many mothers only wake up hours after the baby has been born, too drugged and sleepy to rejoice in the birth of their children. There is not much sense in suffering, since drugs can be given for pain, itching, and other discomforts. The belief has long died that suffering here on earth will be rewarded in Heaven. Suffering has lost its meaning.

Death is like an initiation ceremony, and dying is like a rite of passage from one existence to another. Rites of passage are used partly as a means of preparatory socialization – attitudes and responses undergo a change. Dying is no exception. The living have to cope with two problems: their feelings in the here-and-now for the dying person, and also their feelings about their imminent loss. Soon the patient will no longer exist. Religion is used as an auxiliary help by both patient and survivors. If the people involved have a strong faith in their religious beliefs, the act of dying can be made so much simpler. The Salvation Army, for example, think of the dead as being 'promoted' – presumably to the Army in Heaven. However, most people have to find other ways of dealing with the pains of dying, as religion has lost much of its influence (Kubler-Ross, 1970, pp. 13–14):

> But with this change, also, fewer people really believe in life after death, in itself perhaps a denial of our mortality. Well, if we cannot anticipate life after death, then we have to consider death. If we are no longer rewarded in Heaven for our suffering, then suffering becomes purposeless in itself. If we take part in church activities in order to socialize or to go to a dance, then we are deprived of the Church's formal

53

purpose, namely to give hope, a purpose in tragedies here on earth, and an attempt to understand and bring meaning to otherwise unacceptable painful occurrences in our life.

Usually at some point the doctors dissociate themselves from the dying patient and the nurses only give peripheral attention.[2] The family and friends are trying to come to terms with their own feelings, perhaps with the help of a clergyman. Whilst this is going on the patient has to go through a process of adaptation, too. What happens, of course, will depend on whether he knows that he is dying – for some are never informed. (This also applies sometimes to the family.) Dr Ross has listed five possible stages which the patient might go through in accepting that he is about to die.

First there may be denial and isolation when the patient refuses to accept the facts which the doctors have told him. The isolation refers to the behaviour of the hospital staff – for a variety of reasons they may avoid as much contact as possible with the patient. It would be seen that, in the beginning, most patients use some denial.

The second stage is anger. This can be a particularly difficult stage for anyone who is involved with the patient. This is because the anger is dissipated at random – anyone may become the target at any time. Basically the patient cannot understand why this is happening to him – why shouldn't it be someone else. Next the patient may begin a bargaining stage. Here the usual plea is for more time, or for a very special favour which is usually tied in with the limits placed on the patient by the illness. For example an opera singer who has cancer of the jaw wants to give one final performance.

The patient may possibly become depressed in one of two ways. Either as a reaction to the news or in the realization of his eventual death. Finally the patient may come to accept what is happening, and thus come to terms with death.

When death happens in a family no one can avoid facing it. Everyone has to deal with it in some way or another. The dying person must ultimately come to terms with death quite alone. At some point, the patient can no longer appeal to anyone for help – his isolation is total. The family, too, must undergo a similar readjustment. We initially spoke of death as being an event: so it is, and everyone is in some way affected by it.

Thus death is a very difficult time for everyone concerned. But the difficulties that we have mentioned have often been created and are not necessarily inherent in the situation. Problems have been multiplied by really disturbed patterns of communication – by denial, secrets, fantasy, and confusion. This process would seem to be in direct contradiction to our basic desires. Vilhelm Aubert in his book *The Hidden Society* (1963), says:

> Assuming that death requires social structure and in-learning in order to be accepted, we may view the bed as a training ground for dying. . . . A quiet death, and a dying person's resignation to his inevitable fate, appears to be highly valued by the bereaved ones.

If this is true, and it seems reasonable, then it is important to take positive action in order to make it come true. The taboo on dying must be lifted – we must encourage everyone to share, openly and honestly, all information. This includes not only the family and friends, but the doctors, nurses, the clergy. And, unlike now, the patient must be included in this process. It is only in this way that the process of dying can be made easier, and, perhaps most important, we may learn to come to terms, each of us individually, with our own mortality.

Notes

1 For those interested, further material can be gathered from a very valuable book, Sheldon J. Lachman, *Psychosomatic Disorders: A Behaviouristic Approach*, John Wiley, 1972. For criminals: Howard S. Becker, *Outsiders*, Collier-Macmillan, 1963, and for mental illness, see Thomas Szasz.
2 See Duff and Hollingshead (1968, pp. 66, 217) on the role of the nurse.

2 THE ROYAL FAMILY

Hamlet by William Shakespeare

Inscription on the monument marking Hamlet's grave[1]

AMLED YPPERSTED
OLDTIDS – SNILLE
TEED SIG TAABE
TIL HAEVNENS TIME
KAAREN PAA TING
AF JYDER TIL KONGE
HJSAT HAN HVILER
PAA AWWELHEDE

Translation:
HAMLET HIGH PRIEST
ANCIENT TIMES – GENIOUS
PLAYED THE FOOL
UNTIL (HIS) TIME OF REVENGE
ELECTED TO PARLIAMENT
FROM JUTLANDERS TO KINGS
IN PRAISE HE RESTS
ON THE AMMEL MOORS

Obtained from *Vor Tids Konversations Lexikon*, edited by Jorgen Budtz-Jorgensen, Mag. Art. and Harold W. Moller, Cand. Mag. Aschehoug Danish Publisher, Copenhagen 1942, p. 194:

> AMLED Danish mythical hero. The tale is about how ingenious he was in not living up to his uncle's expectations, the man who had taken his father's life and empire, by pretending madness until he eventually got revenge. The tale was developed in Jutland, Denmark, by taking certain

traits or features from the novel *Sagnverden* (Brutus) and from Eastern (Oriental) mythical tales. (FIRST) recorded by Saxo and through his Latin Danish History, it became known throughout Europe. (The tale) had been dramatized in English prior to Shakespeare using it quite freely in his tragedy *Hamlet*.

For many years, Hamlet's grave was thought to be in Helsingor. Later it was asserted that Amled was buried, supposedly, on the Ammel Moors in Jutland. Here, in September 1933, a monument was unveiled in memory of Amled.

And let me speak to th'yet unknowing world
How these things came about. So shall you hear
Of carnal, bloody, and unnatural acts,
Of accidental judgements, casual slaughters,
Of deaths put on by cunning and forc'd cause,
And, in this upshot, purposes mistook
Fall'n on the inventor's heads. All this can I
Truly deliver.

(p. 137)

From the Renaissance onwards, the character of Hamlet has enjoyed a very special kind of public admiration. It has something to do with the succeeding generations of continuing applause, and the fact that every major critic has paid some kind of respectful homage to him, so elevating him from the status of a fictional creation to that of a sacred institution. There is no doubt that as a character-portrait Hamlet is an exceptional example of the playwright's art, but perhaps his universal popularity is more in debt to a certain quality of the character itself – that of the romantic, soulful, inwardly tormented youth, sensitive, almost too brilliant for his own good, and relentlessly misunderstood and ruthlessly persecuted by the philistines around him. It is not just the passionately committed Shakespearian actor who identifies with this appealing image: many of the most objective and pedantic scholars who have added their comments to the play would secretly like to see themselves cast in the same mould. Samuel Taylor Coleridge is a good example of just such a critic, and it becomes evident on reading his long and detailed analysis of Hamlet's personality that we are being told much more about the

private way Coleridge would like to see himself than we are about
the dramatic character of Hamlet. But then this is all a part of the
Hamlet magic.

Hamlet was first recorded in the early thirteenth century by a
Danish historian called Saxo Grammaticus – the principal vari-
ation between Saxo's *Amleth* and Shakespeare's later stage version
being a happy ending. For while in *Hamlet* the whole family is
slaughtered, Saxo's Amleth returns from England to kill the
villainous uncle-king in a sword fight and then successfully takes
the throne. The story made various appearances in print in the
300 years following Saxo's version, culminating in the production
of an Elizabethan stage play, now with the revised title of *Hamlet*,
and performed with a good degree of popular success some ten or
twenty years before Shakespeare came to write his masterpiece.
All record of this 'shadow' Hamlet has now been lost, including
the name of the author, but many literary speculators strongly
favour Thomas Kyd who wrote, among other things, the *Spanish
Tragedy*, and whose penchant for a good vengeful story-line would
have made much capital of the Hamlet legend.

But would Hamlet be quite so attractive if he were a real
person, living today as one of our contemporaries, and solilo-
quizing about his misfortunes in perhaps a more modern turn of
phrase? Possibly he would have more to complain about if he were
alive today. But certainly it is also possible that the same people
who now admire him so much in the theatre would soon come to
regard him as a most difficult and objectionable young man if they
had dealings with him in real life. And it is even more possible
that in our contemporary climate Hamlet would soon find himself
voluntarily or forcibly referred to a psychiatrist, whose comments
on the favourite son of the English stage would be likely to be in
terms much more prosaic and practical than that of the previous
literary comments which Hamlet has inspired.

Assuming that Hamlet's parents were taking the same stand-
point that they do in the play, and were complaining that
their son was a violently dangerous madman, totally divorced
from his senses, the resultant psychiatric report might read as
follows:

NAME OF PATIENT: Hamlet. STATUS: Prince of Denmark. Male,
30 years of age, Danish. Only child. Introverted personality.
Intellectual and intelligent: IQ 130.

CIRCUMSTANCES: Lives at home with family. Natural father died recently. Mother now re-married to father's brother.

SYMPTOMS: Persistent acute periods of depression, with thoughts of suicide. Depressions alternate with rapid mood-swings to manic elation. Conversation often irrational and nonsensical. Behaviour unpredictable. Liable to sudden unexplained outbursts of rage. Possibly violent. Very hostile and suspicious. Suffers hallucinations involving dead father.

1. I examined the patient in a 30-minute interview. Symptoms consistent with a state of psychosis – e.g. grotesque hallucinations, severe impairment of reality perception, total inability to communicate rationally, poor orientation in time and space: imagines murderous intentions towards him by family and others, and has a rich fantasy life concerned with lurid violence.

DIAGNOSIS: Paranoid Schizophrenic. Potentially very dangerous. Recommend patient's detention under a Section 4 for his own safety and for those around him. Treatment: initial course of 12 ECTSs; 70 mg/day Triptophen, 50 mg/day Librium. If no improvement, Leucotomy may be indicated. Dr WS. 11 July.

2. I examined the patient in a series of three 30-minute interviews over a two-week period. Noted following characteristics: low self-esteem; connected with acute feelings of guilt and a compulsion towards self-accusation and minute analysis of own and others' behaviour. Tendency to intellectualize, particularly on personal issues. Considerable repressed hostility, especially towards stepfather (I suspect Dr WS received some of this transference). Very possessive attitude towards mother. Infantile sexuality. Impaired ability to make and maintain committed relationships, markedly so with opposite sex. Classic symptoms of depression – inertia, low motivation, avowed despair, no goals or personal ambitions.

When engaged at a sympathetic level I found the patient's ability to communicate good, his insight and perception sharp and clear. I did not find him to be schizophrenic within the ordinary meaning of the word. For this reason I am reluctant to agree with Dr WS's diagnosis, doubtless aggravated by acute grief and depression due to real father's recent death. Recommend one-to-one psychotherapy, possibly 2/3 sessions/week.

PSYCHOLOGICAL RESULTS: *TAT findings* indicate excessive dependence upon family, strong protective (poss. sexual?) feelings in regard to the mother, fear and hatred of stepfather, who is seen in terms of a powerful and superior competitor. Subject sees own role in family as passive. Identifies with dead father. Good objective perception for structions outside the family: high objective intelligence, but confused sex attitudes suggest retarded emotional age of 12 or 13.

EEG findings: No evidence of organic damage. Patterns not abnormal under alcohol.

RORSCHACH findings: Images of violence and death repeatedly manifested on tests – subject extremely hostile, possibly violent (? not clear) – natural father's death referred to a number of times – this episode seems to be important in subject's present attitude. Totally unresolved Oedipal feelings. Poor time orientation – completely unable to date father's death.

PROGNOSIS: Poor.

This concocted report is not as far-fetched or fanciful as it might seem. All the observations contained in it are in fact based strictly upon Hamlet's behaviour as recorded in the text of the play, and any modern doctor, faced with such behaviour in the course of his practice, would probably make comments and deductions much like these. What is interesting is that our two imaginary psychiatrists, working from exactly the same limited collection of facts, have come to very different clinical conclusions about the nature of Hamlet's personality. The first doctor says that the man is mad, and should be shut away as a danger to society, while the second says that he is nothing of the sort, that he really is only exceptionally depressed as a result of his father's death. Obviously, these two doctors have very different approaches to their job, when they can arrive at such differences of opinion about the same patient. They also have different ideas about the meaning of effective treatment, as their separate recommendations show. This basic disagreement between two doctors working on the same case is symptomatic of a larger disagreement within the profession. Given a fundamental difference of training and background theory, the surprising difference in attitude quoted above would by no means be unusual in an independent case report.

The psychiatrists give us two different viewpoints on the same theme, and their divided opinion is mirrored by a similar division in literary circles on the subject of Hamlet's sanity. There has been, in the past, considerable controversy between critics for and against the view that Hamlet is mad.

Getting bogged down in this superficial argument is a certain way to lose sight of the important lessons that the play has to teach us about the reactions of vulnerable people under pressure. The problem with the psychiatric report is that the psychiatrists are caught up in the method of diagnosis and symptomology – a method which is no doubt of importance and value to the psychiatrist's elder brother, the medical practitioner, but which in the wider field of human behaviour is more like scientific violin-playing while the patient's condition burns. Faced with the problem of a Hamlet hell-bent on stabbing his stepfather and whoever else might get in the way, it seems pointless to pontificate on whether he is paranoid, or schizophrenic, or just plain murderously angry. What is possibly more important is to look for ways in which the general safety of the family might have been better preserved from the orgy of destruction which eventually engulfs them, to find some reasons for Hamlet's extravagant behaviour in the play, and to suggest ways in which the private problems of the family might have been resolved by means other than murder.

Our starting point is therefore the psychiatric report, which, with its contradictory diagnosis, confused theories, and poor prognosis, is not a very encouraging forecast for Hamlet's future. The report does not go very far towards answering some of the questions that are crucial to Hamlet's well-being and peace of mind; such questions as: how can he honourably pay off what he sees as an overwhelming sense of duty to his dead father's memory? What would killing his stepfather actually solve? And what is his mother's attitude to the outrage that he sees has been committed?

Perhaps we can move away from the psychiatrist's view, first by regarding Hamlet not as necessarily mad, or sane, or schizophrenic, or whatever, but simply as a man with some practical problems. At the time of the play, Hamlet cannot see his problems clearly or objectively, and consequently finding a solution is difficult. Second, the problems are not exclusive to Hamlet. These are problems which involve the other members of his family and to a lesser degree the friends of his family.

Our thesis is that Hamlet is not mad in the legal or clinical sense, but rather that his behaviour is logical in terms of family expectations and interaction in a family system.

Ronald Laing and A. Esterson in their work *Sanity, Madness and the Family* bring into serious question some of the traditional views about the cause of mental illness in general and of schizophrenia in particular. The authors clearly feel that madness is something we create because we cannot tolerate the reality around us.

So it is evident that the story of Hamlet has been an object of fascination over the centuries that preceded Shakespeare: almost, in many ways, like the legend of Oedipus, it had been told and repeated, written and re-written, for the benefit of succeeding generations. And like Oedipus, the tale of Hamlet is weighted with much more seriousness and significance than at first meets the eye. On the surface, the story is primitive, adolescent and unsubtle: the wicked, devious uncle, the tormented son, the blandly innocent mother, extravagant conspiracies of murder, revenge, and retaliation, a royal family battlefield with poisoned chalices being passed around at the dinner table and the fate of a whole nation hanging on the outcome. Rather, as we shall come to see, the significance of the story of Hamlet lies in the family itself and the pain and tragedy which the family creates for itself.

The best way to understand the interaction in *Hamlet* is to read the play as the story of an extended family, with all the members of the court at Elsinore as part of this family. It is not unreasonable to assume that Shakespeare meant the play to be read in this way. The character of a medieval royal court would have been that of a community of relatives, of nephews, cousins, second cousins, uncles and great-uncles, as well as fathers and sons, mothers and daughters. This character of a related community still persists even today in royal circles. In medieval times the King would exercise his royal prerogative in nominating members of his family to court positions, and no one would have dreamed of using the word 'nepotism'. Thus, following this view, we might say that the full 'royal family' at Elsinore consists of eight important members.

The nuclear family consists of:
GERTRUDE, Queen and mother to the family;
CLAUDIUS, the new King and the stepfather;
HAMLET, the son.

Members of the extended family include:

POLONIUS, has always been a kind of counsellor/adviser to the nuclear family, fairly incompetent but has an accepted status, rather an interfering busybody, but well-meaning. As such he is in the position of a bumbling but affectionate uncle;

OPHELIA, daughter to Polonius, lover to Hamlet;

LAERTES, son of Polonius, Ophelia's brother, and a kind of favourite to the King and Queen;

ROSENCRANTZ and GUILDENSTERN, one-time, old contemporary friends of Hamlet;

HORATIO, Hamlet's faithful friend, who despite his faithfulness remains very passive and acts merely as a bystander to the catastrophe that he sees developing.

The rest of this chapter we shall devote to the theoretical analysis of the play itself. The theories which we shall discuss in connection with the royal family are: covert communication, the double-bind, the 'perfect family' myth, the scapegoat syndrome and secrets and their effects upon the family.

Covert communication

Today it is fashionable to question every concept, every idea, all social institutions. It is also the in thing to blame all breakdowns in inter-personal relationships on a breakdown in communication. Union leaders, politicians, diplomats, parents and children who feel the generation gap, newly married couples, and particularly families – all blame poor communication.

Communication is such an important part of our life style that it has even been recognized by the academic world. At the University of California in Los Angeles, a Ph.D. may be earned by anyone who is particularly interested in the mechanics of communication. Communication, written or spoken, can be a very complex affair, or it can be abysmally simple, depending on whether one person really wants the other person to understand or not.

The most primitive communication is that in which actions speak louder than words. You can effectively communicate hatred by punching the person on the nose, just as you can effectively communicate love by touch, embrace, or the sex act. But to elaborate on these two extremes with any sublety, language is

63

necessary. The communicative effectiveness of language is now a separate subject in itself. Such scholars as I. A. Richards, Marshall McLuhan, C. K. Ogden, Edward Sapir, have all made important contributions to the theories of language communication, and the subject as an academic study threatens to sweep an entirely new syllabus into our universities.

Bad communication – that kind of communication which does not convey accurately what the speaker means to say – is an inevitable characteristic of a family in disintegration. The Hamlet family, as we have discussed, is just such a family, and in the play Shakespeare has faithfully recorded the kind of dialogue that we would expect in these circumstances.

Hamlet opens with a short first scene in which the guards on midnight duty on the castle battlements encounter the ghost of Hamlet's dead father. The main value of this scene is as a theatrical ploy – it abruptly captures the audience's interest and imagination, it is very dramatic and foreboding of the direction in which the subsequent action of the play will develop. We shall not spend very much time talking about the ghost or those incidents in which he plays a part. If you were an Elizabethan theatre-goer then the ghost simply was a real ghost who stormed around the battlements on cold winter evenings terrifying the soldiers and shouting 'Remember me!' in the echoing sepulchral tones of a loudspeaker train announcement in Grand Central Station. If you are not superstitious, and you are looking at *Hamlet* from the point of view of psychological interpretation, then the ghost is a device, a symbol representing the guilt of Claudius and Gertrude: and with nothing less than the utmost respect for the ghost himself, for the purpose of this exercise we shall simply ignore his presence and concentrate on the interaction between live family members in the play.

This takes us past scene one into scene two, where we are introduced to all the members of the Hamlet family, together with most of the other people with whom the family has relationships. This scene is the main exposition of the play: and it is here that Hamlet, his mother and stepfather have some of their most important exchanges. The communication in this scene is classic, in that it serves as a beautiful example of how individual members of a family that is on the verge of some kind of collapse can be of vital relevance and importance to the family future, and yet then can talk without saying anything important or relevant at all. There is, as there is in all such families, a complete split between what they say and what they mean (which is a kind of definition of schizophrenia). As a demonstration of this division between sense and meaning we can take the following extract from the family's conversation and lay it out in two columns, thus:

What they say	*What they mean*
KING But now, my cousin Hamlet, and my son,	I would like you to treat me as father.
HAMLET (*aside*) A little more than kin, and less than kind.	I dislike and distrust you, though I would not say so straight to your face.
KING How is it that the clouds still hang on you?	Why are you acting odd? (Though I already know the answer.)
HAMLET Not so, my Lord: I am too much in the sun.	Pointed sarcasm. (Also) I feel guilty about living at all.
QUEEN Good Hamlet, cast thy nighted colour off, And let thine eye look like a friend on Denmark. Do not forever with thy veiled lids Seek for thy noble father in the dust. Thou know'st 'tis common – all that lives must die, Passing through nature to eternity.	Stop grieving about your father and treat your step-father as if you liked him. Don't mourn your father's death, because it bothers us, it makes us feel guilty. Be like us, pretend his death was a natural event.
HAMLET Ay, madam, it is common.	Bullshit. Is it common to first spread butter over mouldy bread?
QUEEN If it be, Why seems it so particular with thee?	I think you are a bit odd if you have such feelings.
HAMLET Seems, madam! Nay, it *is*! I know not 'seems'. 'Tis not alone my inky cloak, good mother, Nor customary suits of solemn black, . . . That can denote me truly. These indeed *seem*, For they are actions that a man might play. But I have that within Which passes show: These but the trappings And the suits of woe.	I *do* have these feelings, they're real and they hurt me. I am very angry as well with the way you two treat my father's death and treat me, but I can only express this anger in bitter speech and indirect hostility, because I am not yet ready to risk my father's fate – I am still not absolutely clear.

65

What they say	*What they mean*
KING 'Tis sweet and commendable in your nature, Hamlet, To give these mourning duties to your father: . . . but to persevere In obstinate condolement is a course Of impious stubbornness; 'tis unmanly grief: It shows a will most incorrect to heaven, . . . An understanding simple and unschool'd. . . . 'Tis . . . a fault to nature, To reason most absurd. . . . This unprevailing woe, and think of us As a father.	Not only are you stupid and obstinate, but you are probably effeminate to be upset about your father. I am *ordering* you to stop expressing your feelings, or else. It is not natural to be upset over a father's death, and if you persist then you will be a misfit not only in the family but to the whole world. Your behaviour threatens me, makes me feel less secure, therefore I want you to treat me as your father because I think that in an affectionate father-son relationship you won't be such a threat to me.

(pp. 11–12)

We might call this technique covert communication – for want of a better term – since the speaker's meaning is concealed by, rather than elucidated by, the words that he uses. It is understandably difficult for anyone on the receiving end of this kind of communication to make clear sense out of what is being said to him – this leads to confusion, which in turn leads to doubt, suspicion and mistrust, all important factors in the disintegration of a family. It requires considerable interpretation to cut through the covering mass of misleading conversation and get to the real issues and real feelings that are involved underneath. What, for example, is Polonius (much abused intruder in the Hamlet family affair) supposed to make of the following exchange with Hamlet?

POLONIUS   My Lord, the queen would speak with you, and presently.

HAMLET   Do you see yonder cloud that's almost in shape of a camel?

POLONIUS   By th'mass, and 'tis like a camel, indeed.

HAMLET   Methinks it is like a weasel.

POLONIUS   It is backed like a weasel.

HAMLET   Or, like a whale?

POLONIUS   Very like a whale.

HAMLET   Then I will come to my mother by and by.   (p. 78)

This strange communication with Polonius serves two purposes for Hamlet: first he tests the old man out to see how he will respond, to see whose side he is on. After Polonius obviously humours him it becomes clear to the Prince that he is collaborating with the King and Queen. When he realizes this, Hamlet becomes hostile and the speech becomes a mockery of the old man. Foolishness, admittedly, is Polonius' speciality, and he does not work very hard at disproving Hamlet's point. But if these manoeuvres do have a deeper meaning, then that meaning is the dislike and contempt which Hamlet has for Polonius: for he sees Polonius as a lackey to the King and Queen, a favour-carrying message-boy whose protests of concern for Hamlet's welfare are not to be trusted. Hamlet could have made the communication much clearer to Polonius by saying honestly what he felt:

POLONIUS   My Lord, the Queen would speak with you, presently.

HAMLET   My Lord, why is it that she cannot tell me this herself. Run off on your errands; go kiss the hand of my King and Queen, and tell them how I am mad, for this you will do whatever I say – will you not? But mark it well, Polonius, that I am far from mad – you mistake for madness my merely being out of favour. And mark also this, Polonius, beware of my anger, for my patience tires marvellously quickly of tedious grey-beards who will run and jump through the hoop of any outrageous lie so that they may curry favour with the King and Queen.

Had Hamlet made this message very clear Polonius might not have died suddenly and unexpectedly on the end of his sword in Act III. For the murder of Polonius is the ridiculous and tragic culmination of a series of misunderstandings that grow out of covert communication. This fatal outcome could have been circumvented by greater honesty and communication on either side – from Polonius to Hamlet. To go back to the camel-weasel-whale exchange, Polonius is so intent in humouring what he believes to be a dangerous madman that it is impossible for him to be honest or straightforward with Hamlet. The word has gone out on Hamlet – 'his wit's diseas'd' – and Polonius has been caught up in the general hysteria. But in humouring Hamlet he is making the worst possible mistake, for as long as he continues to humour him he is not likely to find out whether Hamlet really is mad or not. With this social worker approach he is not in fact likely to find out anything about Hamlet at all. Had he simply been honest in the conversation, and said what was on his mind, then subsequent events might have turned out very differently again:

POLONIUS   My Lord, the Queen would speak with you, presently.

HAMLET   So – like my mother and father – you think I am mad?

POLONIUS   I come to you with a message that the Queen would see you, and you talk to me of clouds and camels. Is this not the very stuff of madness? Such things are wild and senseless, my Lord: they have no meaning for me.

HAMLET   But I am not mad. I speak that way to you because I think of you thus, . . . etc.

Once again a few lines of open communication might have made a colossal difference, and have brought these two men much closer to a sympathetic understanding of each other's problems.

The mechanics of covert communication are basically very simple. Because of complicated fears, a quantity of intense feeling is kept stifled and suppressed. Then it goes on, and while the communication continues on the same level, feigning politeness or protocol in deference to unspoken rules which are never clearly defined anyway, the feelings build up and are bottled up, bursting to be expressed. The limitations of covert communication can no longer contain these enormous pressures, and so dialogue between people begins to break down, taking on that wild and arbitrary character we associate with madness:

HAMLET   Your worm is your only emperor for diet: we fat all creatures else to fat us, and we fat ourselves for maggots: your fat king and your lean beggar is but variable service – two dishes, but to one table: that's the end.

KING   Alas, alas!

HAMLET   A man may fish with the worm that hath eat of a king, and eat of the fish that hath fed of that worm.

KING   What dost thou mean by this?

HAMLET   Nothing but to show how a king may go a progress through the guts of a beggar.

(pp. 93–4)

The King might well exclaim 'alas', for at this juncture Hamlet's words do seem to be the product of an unbalanced mind. But this is because he is trying to say that he hates the king and would like to kill him: covert communication allows no avenue for the expression of such basic feelings as these. But what covert communication in this particular family does allow is for Polonius to spy upon Hamlet, with the King and Queen's authority. Polonius makes a sad error of judgement in allowing himself to become the instrument of the parents' anxiety about their son: sad because it is his activities as the family private detective that lead him to his death. He goes, with the King's special approval, to eavesdrop on a private meeting which Hamlet is to have with his mother in her bedroom – and it is here that Polonius stops Hamlet's rapier with his chest as the end reward for his untiring vigilance and inquiry into other people's affairs. Polonius' death is the not altogether surprising conclusion of the family spying game that has grown up with Hamlet as the main attraction. This family spying game is based on two very strange assumptions, assumptions which make no sense at all when looked at logically but which are none the less not uncommon in certain kinds of families. The first assumption is that Hamlet, the son, has no right to a private life of his own – all his movements are watched and reported on, his love letters to Ophelia are read out in open court. The second assumption is that spying is an effective way of improving the communication with someone in the family whose position is isolated, that it is a justified method of expressing concern or affection. Hamlet himself seems to accept this assumption: he knows that he is being spied upon all the time, but he never as much as says to anyone that he does not care for this game that is being played.

Polonius treats his children in very much the same way. Ophelia has to report her encounters with Hamlet, blow-by-blow, to her father: Polonius sends his servant Reynaldo to spy on his son's activities in Paris. An expert himself in spying on other people's children, Polonius gives his servant the most incredibly detailed briefing on how to investigate Laertes' private life. Shakespeare was obviously intent on pressing home a particular point in this play: for the dominating theme in *Hamlet* is parents and children, and the tragic failure of these two separate camps to make contact with each other.

Double-bind

Don't read this sentence

You have just been placed in the 'infamous' double-bind. In order to register the instruction, you have to read the sentence, and by doing so you expressly disobey what it tells you to do.

The double-bind theory in family therapy is regarded by most family therapists as one of the most valuable pieces of research in the last quarter of a century. In a double-bind situation, the individual is presented with an important piece of communication which actually contains a pair of messages. The conflict arises because the two messages are mutually contradictory – they are of different levels or logical types which are related but incongruent. The recipient of the message is usually unable to respond by leaving the field – in a family often because of the nature of the relationship. Hence it becomes necessary to respond in some way. The difficulty of making an adequate response is obvious, because to do so would mean encompassing both the duality and the contradiction. However, the situation can be further complicated by the fact that accompanying the message is often a concealment or a denial of the inherent contradiction – which means that it is made almost impossible for the recipient to comment on the contradictions involved. What this means in practice is that, first, it is impossible to respond to both messages simultaneously, but, second, if the recipient attempts to follow just one of the messages, he is punished because he denies the other.

Usually the double-bind pattern exists between two people. However, it does happen that three people can be involved. An example of this was clearly demonstrated in the film *Family Life*.[2] In this film we see the 17-year-old daughter chosen as a scapegoat before our eyes. As the story unfolds, we see that Janice can do nothing right. She becomes pregnant, she has the 'wrong' kind of boy friend, she finds it hard to concentrate at work. Finally, she ends up in a mental hospital. During one of the visits, the father tells Janice that she should not be ashamed because she is a patient in a mental hospital. Janice insists she is not ashamed. The mother at this point says, 'That's just the trouble, you should be ashamed.' Here the mother and father operate together to put Janice in a double-bind. In this family, as in most disturbed families, it is easy to imagine what would have happened had Janice attempted to point out the contradictory nature of the parents' communication. Any attempt would simply have met with a barrage of denial, in which Janice would have further suffered by being accused of distrusting or disliking her parents.

Weakland (1960) points out an interesting corollary to the double-bind. It is most obvious in close relationships such as are found in the family. But a parallel situation can be found in a treatment situation between a patient and two individual staff members – who both have different limits and prohibitions which they apply in their relationship with the client. In this way a similar, and obviously equally confusing, situation is created which closely resembles the communication patterns which we are discussing here.

'Don't send anyone into my office to see me when I'm in,' Major Major tells his sergeant on duty at the door. 'If someone comes to see me when I'm in, ask them to wait until I've gone out, then you can send them in to see me.' The duty sergeant in Joseph Heller's *Catch-22* is obviously going to have some difficulties in carrying out this instruction, however conscientiously he tries: if he has to wait until the Major goes out, then he cannot send a visitor into his office to see him, since he is not there. In point of fact he does his best to obey the instruction, with the result that hopeful visitors to the Major's quarters come away with the firm conviction that the sergeant is mad. *Catch-22* has been amongst the most successful and popular novels of the last decade, a brilliant and bitterly funny book whose humour is based very largely upon the particularly irony of the double-bind. In writing it Heller simply coined a new term of his own for an old process of paradoxical communication: instructions are issued which are self-contradictory, and cannot be obeyed. The recipient of the instructions is thereby placed in an impossible situation.

The double-bind is used a number of times as a method of communication in the Hamlet family. There are a number of set pieces which illustrate the double-bind very well, as in the following examples:

1 Claudius tells his stepson Hamlet

. . . think of us
As of a father . . . with no less nobility of love

> Than that which dearest father bears his son
> Do I impart towards you. . . .
> And we beseech you, bend you to remain
> Here, in the cheer and comfort of our eye.
>
> (p. 13)

At the same time he says this, it is apparent that there is very little cheer and comfort in Claudius' eye as far as Hamlet is concerned, and even less of that nobility of love. He is saying that he wants to have a close father-son relationship with Hamlet while his manner and his bearing make it quite clear that he wishes to remain cold, aloof, and unapproachable.

2   The King and Queen as parents ask Hamlet why he is so moody and despondent: 'How is it that the clouds still hang on you?' When Hamlet tells them the reason – his father's recent death – they simply reject this reply out of hand, and persist in asking him the question over and over again in a dozen different ways – by spies, messengers, and ceaseless interrogation at a distance. Hamlet is 'double-bound' by his parents' obstinate inquiry: if he tells them the nature of their question then they will not hear it, and they repeat the question again and again; if he stays silent and says nothing, then they ask their question all the more anxiously.

3   Hamlet stays on in the court at the King's specific request against his initial intention of returning to Wittenburg. Having persuaded Hamlet to stay at home it is only a short time before Claudius is desperate to send him away to England. It is understandable if towards the end of the play Hamlet does not know whether he is coming or going.

4   Polonius starts off by giving his daughter Ophelia a very clear message as regards her relationship with Hamlet:

> I would not, in plain terms, from this time forth,
> Have you so slander any moment's leisure,
> As to give words or talk with Lord Hamlet.
>
> (pp. 22–3)

Three scenes later this same father is making all the arrangements for his daughter to have a special meeting with Hamlet at which she is to talk intimately of their love, for the benefit of Polonius and the King who are spying on them from behind a curtain. From this point on Ophelia is completely confused about what her father is telling her to do. She is (a) *not* supposed to have anything to do with Hamlet, because of her father's basic disapproval of the relationship; and (b) she must have a relationship with Hamlet in order to give her father private information about him which he can then report to the King. The fact that Ophelia eventually goes mad may not be totally unrelated to this impossible double-bind which her father sets upon her love life.

In literature we can find numerous other examples of this principle. We have selected two, from D. H. Lawrence's *Women in Love*, and Robert Bolt's *A Man For All Seasons* to further demonstrate the double-bind and its possible consequences in relationships.

In *Women in Love* (1945 edn, pp. 371–2), the scene takes place in a ski lodge in Switzerland between Gerald and his mistress Gudrun. Their relationship is on the point of breaking up. Gudrun is alone in her bedroom. Gerald arrives. She puts her hand on his knee and takes his hand:

'Are you regretting Ursula?' he asked.

'No, not at all,' she said. Then in a slow mood, she asked: 'How much do you love me?'

'If only I could kill her,' his heart was whispering repeatedly. 'If only I could kill her – I should be free.'

It seemed to him that death was the only severing of this Gordian knot.

'Why do you torture me?' he said.

She flung her arms around his neck.

'Ah, I don't want to torture you,' she said pityingly, as if she were comforting a child. The impertinence made his veins go cold, he was insensible. She held her arms round his neck, in a triumph of pity. And her pity for him was cold as stone, its deepest motive was hate for him, and fear of his power of her, which she must always counterfoil.

'Say you love me,' she pleaded. 'Say you will love me for ever – won't you?'

But it was her voice only that coaxed him. Her senses were entirely apart from him, cold and destructive of him. It was her overbearing will that insisted.

'Won't you say you'll love me always?' she coaxed. 'Say it, even if it isn't true – say it Gerald, do.'

'I will love you always,' he repeated in real agony, forcing the words out.

She gave him a quick kiss.

'Fancy you actually having said it,' she said with a touch of raillery.

He stood as if he had been beaten.

And in a way he was beaten. If he says he loves her, as he was made to do, he is forced to lie about it because he doesn't really love her. If he refuses to say he loves her, he runs the risk of losing her. What are Gerald's alternatives? He can either be true to himself and keep his integrity and lose Gudrun, which he does not want to do. Or, he can give in and submit, say he loves her and betray himself. We note also his desire to 'kill' Gudrun. In the novel, he actually attacks her twice, something she sets up, but he never carries it off.

In Bolt's play, it is the Chancellor Thomas More who is placed in a double-bind by the King, Henry VIII. After selecting him to be Chancellor, Henry places More in an impossible position:

HENRY   Yes, yes. (*He turns, his face set.*) Touching this other business, mark you, Thomas, I'll have no opposition.

MORE   Your Grace?

HENRY   No opposition I say! No opposition! Your conscience is your own affair; but you are my Chancellor! There, you have my word – I'll leave you out of it. But I don't take it kindly, Thomas, and I'll have no opposition! I see how it will be; the Bishops will oppose me. The full-fed hypocritical, 'Princes of the Church!' Ha! As for the Pope! Am I to burn in Hell because the Bishop of Rome with the Emperor's knife at his throat, mouths me Deuteronomy! Hypocrites! They are all hypocrites! Mind they do not take you in, Thomas! Lie low if you will, but I'll brook no opposition – no words, no signs, no letters, no pamphlets – mind that, Thomas – no writings against me!

MORE   Your Grace is unjust. I am your Grace's loyal minister.

Here we see the beginning of the double-bind. The King tells More that he will leave him out of the situation but at the same time tells More that he will brook no opposition. Later in the play the double-bind becomes solidified and all exits for More are blocked. It would be fascinating to see what a modern statesman would do with the dilemma if he were presented with it today. Note the following passages (pp. 33, 69–70):

CROMWELL   Sir Thomas More, is there anything you have to say to me concerning the King's marriage with Queen Anne?

MORE   I understood I was not to be asked that again.

CROMWELL   Evidently you understood wrongly. These charges . . .

MORE (*anger breaking through*)   They are terrors for children, Mr Secretary, not for me!

CROMWELL   Then know that the King commands me to charge you in His name with great ingratitude! And to tell you that there never was nor could be so villainous a servant nor so traitorous a subject as yourself!

MORE   So I am brought here at last.

CROMWELL   Brought? You brought yourself to where you stand now.

MORE   Yes. Still, in another sense, I was brought.

CROMWELL   Oh yes. You may go home now. For the present. (*Exit More.*) I don't like him as well as I did. There's a man who raises the gale and won't come out of harbour.

RICH   Do you still think you can frighten him?

CROMWELL   No, he's misusing his intelligence.

RICH   What will you do now, then?

CROMWELL   Oh, be quiet, Rich. . . . We'll do whatever is necessary. The King's a man of conscience and he wants Sir Thomas More to bless his marriage or Sir Thomas More destroyed. Either will do.

RICH   They seem odd alternatives, Secretary.

CROMWELL   Do they? That's because you are not a man of conscience. If the King destroys a man, that's proof to the King that it must have been a bad man, the kind of man a man of conscience *ought* to destroy – and of course a bad man's blessing's not worth having. So either will do.

At this point More has no free choices – he cannot even resign his position, because such an action would be interpreted by the rest of the world as open disapproval of the King's decision to obtain a divorce in order to marry Anne Boleyn. Thus the double-bind is firmly locked on two levels: first, the King selected More because of his integrity and honesty. This personal part is reflected in the public business of government – people look to the decision that More will make, because they know that he is honest and sincere. And by the time the accusation is made by Cromwell, the Chancellor is in a hopeless position. First, on a private level, the King demands his acquiesence – which would mean being false to his own conscience, demeaning himself before the King. And also it would mean losing his reputation at the public level.

Thus, for More, the choices presented to him are – agree with the King's demands and forfeit honour, trust and reputation; or disagree with the King and forfeit life. It would indeed be fascinating to see how any statesman would handle such a situation. More's choice is well known. He was executed.

As we have seen from the above examples, a double-bind always makes the individuals involved very unhappy, and sometimes may even have tragic consequences when it is a persistent part of the relationship. This is because a double-bind locks both members into its pattern: the only way it can be unlocked constructively is through the intervention of an outsider – such as a family therapist.

The 'perfect family' myth

There is no such thing as a perfect family. Families are never static, they are forever changing. If one thinks of a mobile, where a part of the mobile may be added or subtracted, you will see that the mobile does not remain still but constantly sways back and forth. In a sense this happens to families when an event such as marriage, illness, birth or death takes place.

More often than not, families tend to be romantic when they talk about their own family. It is not uncommon to hear families refer to themselves as 'the perfect family' except that they are seated in the office of a therapist and complaining about their 'sick' child or 'bad' boy. An article in the London *Sunday Times* magazine was devoted to Core Haven, America's honeymoon capital where the couple pay 400 dollars a week for an opportunity to get to know each other in the most intimate way. For example a dinner is served at 5 p.m. which presumably gives the couple the rest of the evening to indulge in love-making. It is interesting to note that the article made no mention that the resort provided anything like marriage counsellors as part of its staff, possibly because this would put a dent into the romantic picture.

It is only when the honeymoon is over and the couple are faced with the realities of two people living together and seeing each other every day that the concept of the 'perfect family' myth starts to break down. In America, because there is no royal family, there is a tendency to idealize famous families, as was the case with the Kennedys. But even the idealized family can be shattered by the unexpected. Note what happened when death in the form of violent murder came to John F. Kennedy. The event catapulted Lyndon Johnson into power, and it forced Jackie Kennedy to move and find a new home for herself and two children. Later, she remarried, to a powerful figure in the world of finance, Aristotle Onassis, and moved to Greece to learn a new language and culture.

More and more working therapists are coming to treat the phenomena of the deviant, not as the breakdown of an individual (as psycho-analysis does) but as the breakdown of a whole family. In black Africa, a culture one would not normally think to look to for new developments in the sophisticated field of psychotherapy, this approach is commonplace, and the therapist brings in the deviant's whole family for treatment as a matter of course. Not so in Western Europe. There is some strong resistance to this modestly sensible idea, partly because so much of our psychotherapy is founded upon the traditional philosophy and treatment methods of psycho-analysis.

For example, the criminal or alcoholic *does* get unhappy when you call his family into the treatment room to talk about their problems in the family context. And the whole family gets even unhappier when they are posed with such relevant questions as what do they get from having the deviant himself in that special role. But that unhappiness is all right; for it is in that atmosphere of unhappiness and high tension that we can maybe, hopefully, start to work with some of the real problems, and start to effect some change upon the way that these unfortunate people deal with their difficult lives.

For example, in the Hamlet family, members communicate

with their relatives in a progressively wilder and more irrational fashion, until it begins to look as if the whole court at Elsinore have taken leave of their senses. They begin with a single-minded conviction that they must find someone to blame for their troubles, and from this they quickly discover the advantages, for them, in the 'get Hamlet' game – a game whose conclusion is the destruction of them all.

It sounds like nothing less than a sick man's nightmare. But it is, unfortunately, a nightmare which is all too real, as time and again the clients of contemporary family therapy prove to us. You might say, justifiably, that we do not encounter in present day family treatment many royal families in which the brother has murdered the King and married the Queen, and in which the son plots at the stepfather's death, while the stepfather conversely plots at the son's death, and in which the whole bunch end up by killing each other in a kind of mass family suicide. Perhaps families no longer have such a sense of style as they did in medieval times. But families do still have their guilty secrets, their mutual conspiracies, their ineffective communication, their hidden hurtful and hurting feelings whose repression threatens a more dangerous and damaging indirect pain on their other relatives. Families in trouble – those families with which conjoint family therapy (as well as Shakespeare) is concerned – still have that identical sense of sorrow and despair, and they still have their individual members who will deal with the family feelings by becoming delinquents, alcoholics, schizophrenics, or even murderers. Families – in the way that *Hamlet* accurately illustrates them – have not really changed that much over the intervening years; medieval, Elizabethan or twentieth-century – the music may sound a little different but the tune is essentially the same. And sometimes even the reality of that catastrophic last scene in *Hamlet* does not seem that far removed from the perils of modern family life. In 1967 in Wisconsin, Jim McBair killed his wife, his sister-in-law, a friend, and the family baby sitter; a year earlier Charles Joseph Whitman stabbed his wife and mother to death and went to kill fourteen people on the Texas University campus. Every year, thousands who live in the family and who eventually come to find the strain unbearable commit suicide, while thousands more injure, maim or kill their relatives as the climax to some petty family quarrel.

More usually, family problems are expressed in less spectacular and tragic consequences. But while the way in which each family handles its problems varies according to the difference between individual temperaments, those problems themselves remain irrevocably the same. Most people, for example, may fantasize at one time or another in their lives about killing one or all of the members of their family, but fortunately for society, those murderous instincts are rarely acted out. The feeling of rage and resentment is dealt with, or partially dealt with, by the occasional timely family row in which people can shout and scream and give vent to some of their suppressed anger verbally.

The family has traditionally been and still is the nucleus of our society in the way that it works. This is the playground where most people's ideas, insights, and misconceptions about what relating to others is all about are developed and tested.

If you search for a reason for the deviant's unhappy behaviour, then you need look no further than the family where he learns his lessons in behaviour and communication. This was the case for those Elizabethans who saw in *Hamlet* a special kind of truth about the way destructive families operate, and that truth in *Hamlet* remains equally applicable today. Families with unsolved problems tend for the most part to resist most strongly any admission of this truth. And, sadly enough, most of these families who make the effort of starting in treatment, present the therapist (at least in the initial interview) with exactly the same question that Hamlet's parents ask, and in the same tone of hurt and indignant surprise:

> And can you by no drift of conference
> Get from him why he puts on this confusion,
> Grating so harshly all his days of quiet
> With turbulent and dangerous lunacy?

(p. 58)

The answer to this question can only come from within the family itself, in the same way that the solution to the problem can only come from within the family, by means of self-elected change and self-inspired growth.

But if the family elects to resist change, and to preserve the *status quo* of bad communication and dangerous misunderstandings, then they must build themselves a defence against any outside influence which might threaten their equilibrium.

In practice, the 'Perfect Family' myth is just such a defence, it is a mechanism for protecting the family from the fact that they are all really rather odd, and that each of them has special problems which they don't want to deal with. As long as they can go on saying that 'we are the perfect family except for HIM . . .' they need not face the fact that they have these special problems.

An example of this is a family we worked with a number of years ago. The family consisted of father, mother, 18-year-old daughter (the 'model child') and a 16-year-old son. The family stated that it had no problems, that it was in effect a 'perfect family'. After four sessions with the father, who spent most of his time looking out of the window and answered very few questions, he finally was able to disagree with his wife, something which he said he never did. This was the beginning of a family secret which had never been discussed, something which was separate and distinct from the children; a major problem which was part of the parental relationship. After two more sessions, he was finally able to talk about his wife's alcoholism rather than blame his 16-year-old son for being truant from school. In this way the family was able to face some of its real problems and no longer had to defend itself and weave a web of fantasy about being the 'perfect family'.

We are faced with a similar situation when we look at the royal family: for although they never actually say the famous cliché in so many words, they repeat the implication over and over again in their attitude towards their errant son: there is nothing wrong with us, but what is the matter with you? Hamlet's mother says to him very early on:

Why seems it so particular with thee?

She is talking about the death of Hamlet's father. The death of fathers, she says, is a common phenomena, so why should it be bothering Hamlet so much? After all, his father had been dead for nearly two months now. Hamlet's stepfather, Claudius, argues along much the same lines. The two of them appear to find it totally incredible that anyone can mourn the death of a father for longer than a few weeks. As Claudius puts it:

'Tis sweet and commendable in your nature, Hamlet,
To give these mourning duties to your father:
                    . . . but to persevere

In obstinate condolement is a course
Of impious stubbornness, . . .

(p. 12)

It is obvious that it is the whole family that is odd, rather than Hamlet himself. The entire attitude adopted by Gertrude and Claudius in this affair is distinctly less than healthy. Far from any reasonable sympathetic response, their reaction is one of amazement and total disbelief; and they stand aghast at their son. Not only are they amazed, but it is apparent that they see Hamlet's gesture of grief as some kind of personal threat to themselves. 'Fie!' says Claudius

. . . 'tis a fault to heaven,
A fault against the dead, a fault to nature,
To reason most absurd, . . .

(p. 13)

Now the display of grief in a man whose father is but two months dead may be many things, but a 'fault of nature' it most certainly is not. Hamlet's behaviour is at fault, according to Gertrude and Claudius, simply because they do not like it. For devious personal reasons of their own (which we can look at in more detail later) they want to see all remembrance of Hamlet Senior and of his untimely death buried with the body. Because they are themselves abnormal, the family response to Hamlet's behaviour is to define him as mad. To a man with no sense of smell someone who enthuses over the scent of roses may well be different or difficult to understand, but if he then goes further than this and labels a sense of smell as abnormal then he is simply refusing to take account of his own disabilities. Gertrude and Claudius are like people with no sense of smell. If something is rotten in the state of their family then they stop their noses against the stench, and blandly go around remarking how peculiar it is to see other people wrinkling their noses in distaste.

The facts then are rather the opposite of what is suggested by the myth which grows up and comes to be accepted as a truism in the royal family. The myth is that all the rest of the family are in good shape except for Hamlet, who is the delinquent 'black sheep' and whose conduct has little or nothing to do with the lives of those around him. The facts, on the other hand, indicate that the

81

private behaviour of the King, the Queen and Polonius is much
more seriously and dangerously disturbed than anything Hamlet
could hope to aspire to. But the myth protects their private lives
from too close a scrutiny. The assumption is that as long as everyone is caught up in the game of running around watching Hamlet
the so-called madman, then they will be too preoccupied to give
much attention to or look too closely at the behaviour of anyone
else in the family:

KING   Welcome dear Rosencrantz and
                       Guildenstern! . . .
    The need we have to use you did provoke
    Our hasty sending. Something have you heard
    Of Hamlet's transformation: so I call it,
    Sith nor th'exterior nor the inward man
    Resembles that it was. What it should be,
    More than his father's death, that thus hath
                       put him
    So much from th'understanding of himself,
    I cannot dream of. I entreat you both,
           . . . by your companies
               . . . to gather
    So much as from occasion you may glean,
    Whether aught, to us unknown, afflicts him
                      thus,
    That, open'd, lies within our remedy.

                                   (p. 38)

GUILDENSTERN   . . . we both obey, . . .
    Heavens make our presence and our practices
    Pleasant and helpful to him!
QUEEN   Ay, Amen.

                                   (p. 39)

It would have been diplomatic of Rosencrantz and Guildenstern to have stopped and asked themselves whether it was possible
that it was the King and Queen who were the neurotic ones, rather
than Hamlet, and to have made a few discreet inquiries to that
end. Had they done this, they would have discovered the clue to
Hamlet's 'turbulent and dangerous lunacy' in the much more pro-
foundly turbulent and dangerous lunacy of the family. But such

sensible curiosity never occurs to Rosencrantz and Guildenstern simply because they are caught up in the deception of images. Claudius' image is that of an efficient king, a skilful diplomat, confident and adept at guiding his country through the stormy seas of international politics, while at home he is the good family man, loving and considerate of his wife, generous and attentive towards his stepson:

> For let the world take note,
> You are the most immediate to our throne,
> And with no less nobility of love
> Than that which dearest father bears his son
> Do I impart toward you. . . .
>
> (p. 13)

The image of Gertrude is of a discreet queen, tactfully standing back to let her husband take decisions and exercise most of the authority, leaving the politics to the men, but contributing and giving support where there are domestic issues at stake, like a good wife and mother should. Because she and her husband are the ideal parents – for so their joint image presents itself to the casual onlooker – they are justly concerned about the welfare of their son, who it seems is going mad. They handle him kindly but firmly, they show him all the care and attention any son could wish for, they try to do all they can to understand what is troubling him. They call in his old friends Rosencrantz and Guildenstern to give him some nice company, they indulge his whims by letting him put on small plays for court entertainment, and they enlist the further help of Ophelia, his girl-friend, and Polonius her father in order that they might learn what is upsetting him so much, and thereby do something to help him. Their loving patience and tolerance knows no ordinary bounds; it is only when Hamlet kills Polonius for no reason whatsoever, in a fit of complete madness, that they decide he must be sent away to England for his own good and for the general safety of the court.

'Can any son ever have such paragons as parents?' But turn away from this image for the moment, which is a total sham anyway, and look at the reality which lies behind what an American psychiatrist has aptly described as the 'mask of sanity'. Behind that urbane mask which Claudius wears with such aplomb lurks a desperately deranged personality, a personality which would

83

probably nowadays be defined as psychotic, or as near to psychotic as makes little difference. Claudius is a man whose whole thinking has been consumed and destroyed by a terrible, urgent jealousy of quite extraordinary dimensions. To take account of his background is to understand something of his special madness. His life has been a process of growing up with unfavourable comparisons between himself and his brother (Hamlet Senior – Hamlet's late father):

> My father's brother, but no more like my father than I to
> Hercules!
>
> (p. 14)

Hamlet himself of course is bound to be prejudiced, but all the evidence of Claudius' character would seem to indicate that Hamlet's disparaging descriptions of him are close enough to the truth to satisfy most people:

> A murderer and a villain;
> A slave that is not twentieth part the tithe
> Of your precedent lord; a vice of kings;
> A cut-purse of the empire and the rule,
> That from a shelf the precious diadem stole.
> And put it in his pocket!
>
> (p. 86)

A trifle harsh, perhaps, but nothing if not accurate; for Claudius is a murderer and a villain, and, for special reasons of his own, conspired unscrupulously to steal the rightful possessions of his brother.

In order to understand the motives of this murderer and villain you must imagine, in the time that preceded the action of the play, two brothers whose temperaments are seen by all around them to be totally different, and whose relationship bears more than a passing resemblance to the Biblical story of Cain and Abel. Hamlet Senior, is the 'good' brother: nowadays we might use such terms as 'well-adjusted' or 'integrated' to describe him, just as we would probably substitute 'sick' or 'disturbed' in place of 'bad' or 'evil'. This aside, Hamlet Senior has the hallmark of a very successful man. In his professional life, he has come to the highest position of political power in the land, and he has been, it would seem, a most competent and able king, much admired and respected by all who knew him:

> . . . our valiant Hamlet –
> For so this side of our known world esteemed him –
>
> (p. 6)

These are not his son's words, who waxes so eloquently on the subject of his father, but Horatio's, whom we can rely on as an impartial observer. Once again, young Hamlet's description of his relatives seems to have a certain essential accuracy. As for Hamlet Senior's private life, he has married a very attractive and desirable woman, he has a highly intelligent and sensitive son and up until the time of his brother's intervention he would appear to have had a very stable, warm and affectionate family relationship:

> So excellent a king . . .
>   so loving to my mother
> That he might not beteem the winds of heaven
> Visit her face too roughly. . . .
>   Why, she would hang on him,
> As if increase of appetite had grown
> By what it fed on.
>
> (p. 14)

Claudius, the other side of the family coin, is the 'bad' brother. He has neither Hamlet Senior's political abilities nor his capacity for relationships. Like Cain, he finds that his natural gifts are wanting by comparison with his brother. And like Cain, he eventually kills his brother out of the monstrous jealousy and resentment he bears against him for this difference. Having killed his successful brother, he then proceeds to take over the very trappings of his brother's success. Of all the positions of power in the court that he could have aspired to none can satisfy him save his brother's crown, and of all the attractive women in Denmark, none can qualify so well to be his mate as his brother's wife, Gertrude. He even tries to take over Hamlet Senior's role of the loving father:

> We pray you . . . think of us
> As of a father. For let the world take note,
> You are the most immediate to our throne;

85

And with no less nobility of love
Than that which dearest father bears his son
Do I impart toward you.

(p. 13)

This speech, remember, is from the man who has just killed
Hamlet's father, who has been married to his mother for scarcely
a month, and already Hamlet is his well-loved son. To call him,
as Hamlet does, 'a little more than kin and less than kind', is a
masterpiece of under-description: just how kind and loving he is
towards his stepson can be judged from the remaining action of
the play, in which he conspires deliberately and painstakingly at
Hamlet's death. It is almost, in many ways, as if Claudius has
taken over the personality of the brother whom he has murdered:
loving father, considerate husband, now suddenly also the super-
efficient king and diplomat, dispatching timely ambassadors to
Norway and averting the threat of imminent war with the belli-
gerent young Fortinbras, who as a result:

Makes vow before his uncle never more
To give th'assay of arms against your majesty.

(p. 40)

But Claudius in reality is none of the things he appears to be,
neither efficient king, considerate husband nor loving father. In
reality he is a dangerous psychotic, a jealous madman who has
already killed once and who is quite prepared to kill again if he
feels sufficiently threatened.

It would be highly relevant in our consideration of the 'perfect
family' if we were to look closely at Gertrude, and examine her
role in the family. One is tempted at first to dismiss her as nothing
more than a short-sighted and exceptionally stupid woman, save
that there is a strong suggestion throughout the dense and closely-
written text of this play that she knows much more about what is
really happening in her family than she is prepared to admit. She
plays a part that is played by a lot of mothers in families where
unusually difficult and dangerous emotional problems begin to
make themselves felt: she plays the 'dumb mother' role, the 'I
can't understand what all the fuss is about' type of woman who
copes with the reality of the situation by simply pretending that it
does not exist. She colludes with Claudius in their initial total

amazement that Hamlet is still in mourning two months after his father's death, and she manages to come out with the most devasting clichés about the effects of death in the face of Hamlet's genuine grief:

QUEEN Do not forever with thy vailéd lids
Seek for thy noble father in the dust:
Thou know'st 'tis common – all that lives must die,
Passing through nature to eternity.
HAMLET Ay, madam, it is common.
QUEEN   If it be,
Why seems it so particular with thee?

(p. 12)

Being as she is Hamlet's natural mother, and having much greater knowledge than Claudius about the kind of regard in which Hamlet held his late father, there is much less excuse for this response in Gertrude. Whenever she has to deal with the problems of Hamlet's behaviour she assumes a plaintive air of bafflement, whereas privately, in an aside to her new husband, she may confide her opinion of her 'son's distemper' as:

I doubt it is no other but the main:
His father's death, and our o'er hasty marriage

(p. 40)

In one short sentence, she has defined the exact reason for all Hamlet's sullenness, suspicion and resentment: yet still she continues elsewhere to act as if his behaviour made no sense to her at all. The events which have so upset Hamlet would arouse anyone's suspicions. The father of the family dies very suddenly and mysteriously; his wife, until that time apparently devoted to her husband, shows little sign of grief at his premature death; within four weeks she is married to his brother Claudius, a scheming devious individual with few, if any, of Hamlet Senior's virtues to commend him. It requires no Sherlock Holmes to put two and two together and to come to the glaringly obvious conclusion that Claudius has had something to do with his brother's conveniently sudden death – for reasons of his own again; and that Gertrude, if not actually a party to the murder, certainly knows what has happened. In the famous scene where Hamlet confronts her alone in her chamber, he as good as challenges her directly with the truth:

HAMLET   . . . almost as bad, good mother,
         As kill a king and marry with his brother.
QUEEN   As kill a king!

(p. 83)

This parrot repetition of Hamlet's words is the sum total of Gertrude's reaction to the accusation. When Hamlet some lines later emphasizes his statement by referring to Claudius as 'a murderer and a villain', Gertrude's sole response is to cry 'No more!' She does not ask what he means by saying 'as kill a king and marry with his brother'. She does not even make an effort to deny it. In fact, her only words are tantamount to an admission of guilt:

               O Hamlet! speak no more;
   Thou turn'st mine eyes into my very soul;
   And there I see much black and grained spots
   As will not leave their tinct.

(p. 85)

But it is characteristic that she phrases this admission in a request for Hamlet to 'speak no more'. What she says, in effect is 'well, all right, if you're going to get so heated about it, let's not discuss it any more. Whatever happens, this is a subject we must not talk about.' And she has such a capacity for double-think and denial that she is later able to tell Claudius, in description of this interview, that Hamlet was merely

   Mad as the sea and wind, when both contend
   Which is the mightier.

(p. 90)

Gertrude is a woman with a very passive personality; and like a lot of very passive women she defends herself from intimate or hurtful truths by silence and by a kind of blank, guileless *naïveté*. She makes relationships with men who will take all responsibility for her, and who will take care of all necessary arrangements and will bear all the consequences for whatever happens afterwards. Her first husband was a man with a great deal of authority, a man who was strong enough to do his job of running the country and then to come home and be able to carry the weight of his dependent family (for Hamlet also is a very dependent person who eschews the very idea of personal responsibility) entirely on his shoulders.

Gertrude's second husband, Claudius, is likewise a very strong and authoritative figure – whatever else his faults Claudius does take responsibility for the whole shooting match. The fact that Hamlet Senior was a man with a very well defined moral sense of right and wrong, and that Claudius has no morality whatsoever, makes very slight difference to Gertrude, just as long as she has a man upon whom she can depend entirely to take responsibility for her. Hamlet accuses her of having no discrimination in choosing her men:

> . . . what judgement
> Would step from this to this? Sense, sure, you have,
> Else could you not have motion. But, sure, that sense
> Is apoplex'd; for madness would not err,
> Nor sense to ecstacy was ne'er so thralled
> But it reserved some quantity of choice,
> To serve in such a difference.

(p. 85)

And in this respect Hamlet is right. Gertrude shows no active judgment, takes no decisions, gives no advice, because it is important for her to remain in an entirely passive role; things are done to her rather than by her, she is a victim of circumstances rather than in control of the circumstances as she should be, and even if the most outrageous crimes are committed on her behalf along the way, she simply pulls down the steel protective shutter in her mind and pretends that none of these things have happened.

Gertrude's image and Gertrude's reality – it is possible to see how large is the distance which separated the two. It is hardly less so for Claudius. They would present themselves as the ideal mother and stepfather, while underneath their outward poise and calm they are confused, desperate, and dangerously frightened. This difference is the difference between the 'perfect family' myth as it is advertised to unwitting spectators and the contrasting imperfect family members themselves.

The Hamlet family like any modern family is not perfect. We

see that the mythology of the 'perfect family' is destroyed: not only that, but like many a modern family that has a daughter or son in a mental hospital or prison, Hamlet's family never squarely faces the issue and goes on to death and destruction as a way of dealing with the hidden problems.

The scapegoat syndrome

The theory of the scapegoat syndrome is in essence no more complicated than a simple dictionary definition of the word – someone who takes the blame for another's misdeeds. 'Scapegoat' comes originally from the Jewish religion: an annual ceremony was held in which the high priest laid all of the sins of his people upon a goat. The unfortunate animal, probably none the wiser for its sudden symbolic burden, was then sent out into the wilderness, by which exile the tribe was relieved of its year's accumulation of guilt.

The use of the scapegoat symbolism seems to have been a recurring theme in older societies. In ancient Greece the ceremony was not restricted to the animal: in the Festival of the Thargelia, human beings were selected for this role. In Athens, for example, after an animal sacrifice on the Acropolis, two people, chosen primarily because of their deformities, were paraded around the city before being stoned outside the gates. The 'Pharmakoi' – as the victims were called – thus symbolically cleansed the city of its evil. In Babylon a goat was used in this way to cleanse the temple – it was beheaded, and its body rubbed against the walls of the temple to cleanse the impurities left there; its body was then disposed of by being thrown in the river (Woodhouse and Dynely Prince, pp. 218–23).

As used by the exponents of the conjoint family therapy, practically every family has a scapegoat at one time or another. It depends on how much scapegoating is done and whether or not the family is conscious that this is being done to a particular family member. Some families need a member to be delinquent or crazy. In this way the rest of the family can go about its business and pretend that nothing else is wrong with the family. One hears a mother or father say: 'If only Johnny were not such a bad boy, we would have a perfect family.' The fact is that Johnny is often needed to remain bad because he serves as a protective device for the rest of the family. He can cover up the fact that possibly wife and husband have not slept together for ten years, or he can help to hide other kinds of skeletons that threaten to come out of the family closet.

Scapegoating is not only used by families to avoid looking at some real issues that are taking place within the family context. It is a device widely used by politicians to hide political skeletons, by businessmen who have been caught in a crooked deal, by medical people who may be trying to bury their mistakes, when a man-made physical disaster such as fire occurs – all these people have one thing in common, someone must take the blame and that someone is usually somebody that is not always in a position to defend himself. For example: at the tragic night club fire, the Coconut Grove in Boston, Massachusetts in 1942, where 500 people lost their lives (mostly because of panic), the fire inspector was finally indicted and went to prison for two years. It may be argued that the real culprits were the customers who panicked and fell over each other in the rush to get out.

Scapegoats in a family are selected, though they cannot usually be exiled quite so easily to a handy wilderness as they were in ancient Israel – though mental hospitals and prisons are probably the next best thing in our contemporary culture.

In the tenth century, England was far enough removed from Denmark to be seen as something of an undiscovered country whose bourne no traveller returns from: it is to England therefore that the royal family eventually decide to send their scapegoat son when he starts to get out of control:

> I have a quick determination
> Thus set it down: he shall with speed to England,
> For the demand of our neglected tribute:
> Haply the seas and countries different,
> With variable objects shall expel
> This something-settled matter in his heart,
> Whereon his brains still beating puts him thus
> From fashion of himself.

(p. 64)

A good understanding of the scapegoat syndrome, as it applies to the royal family, is fundamental to a better understanding of the play, and it helps to explain many of the peculiarities and obscurities in the action (or inaction, for *Hamlet* is in the main a play of waiting and watching).

The King and Queen have a particularly unpleasant murder on their consciences. Naturally neither of them wants to admit to the crime and have to take the consequences of it. Perhaps less naturally, their guilt is such that they are not even prepared to acknowledge the crime to each other or to themselves. As far as they are concerned, the subject of Hamlet Senior's death is now a closed book. They have decided to deal with their guilt by blanking out from mind and memory. And if they cannot go as far as to pretend that the death never actually happened, then at least they can try to play down its significance, they can make it into a trifling event, a mere commonplace, not worthy of a second thought:

> Thou know'st 'tis common; all that lives must die,
> Passing through nature to eternity.

(p. 12)

In this respect, Hamlet the son is a real thorn in his parent's side. He has a persistent and irritating habit of drawing a blaze of attention to those matters which they wish to draw a discreet curtain over. The very way he presents himself is like a newspaper headline on the subject of his father's death, proclaiming the twin titles of Grief and Suspicion to all and sundry in the court. Worse even than that, he reminds his parents of their own guilt every time they see him with his 'customary suits of solemn black' and 'dejected 'haviour of the visage'. Obviously they have to put a stop to this, one way or the other. So what they do is to serve him with an ultimatum: either you change your behaviour and make light of your father's death as we do, or else we hang a label on you for all to see – 'turbulent and dangerous lunacy'. If someone is publishing slanderous comments about you, then what you do is to discredit the source of the slander. By making Hamlet a madman, his parents totally discredit anything he might possibly have to say about his father's death. Thereafter, when anyone encounters Hamlet, and he is brooding on his deceased father, they say to themselves 'O God, it's his obsession again', and they proceed to 'humour' his madness.

Shakespeare makes it very clear in the play that at the centre of all the hysteria Hamlet himself is uncommonly sane, and remains so throughout, despite whatever the family around him may choose to think. His private conversations with Horatio – cool, considered debates – serve as a periodic reminder of this fact. The shrewdness and accuracy of his observations on other people again point to his essential sanity. He is very alive and sensitive to the intentions of those with whom he comes into contact, and he can call the bluff of a would-be sympathizer's false concern with disconcerting insight and wit:

> You would play upon me; you would seem to know my
> stops; you would pluck out the heart of my mystery . . . and
> there is much music, excellent voice, in this little organ, yet
> cannot you make it speak. 'Sblood, do you think I am easier
> to be played on than a pipe?

> (pp. 77–8)

Yet despite all this, it remains undeniable that Hamlet does take considerable pains to put on a show of madness, in some instances quite convincingly. Having been presented with his family's ultimatum, he wrestles with his conscience (in the shape of the Ghost) for two following scenes, then takes his crucial decision which is confided to Horatio and Marcellus:

> As I perchance hereafter shall think meet
> To put an antic disposition on,

> (p. 32)

By this statement, he has embraced the role of scapegoat which his family have prepared for him. And in the remainder of the play he proceeds to prove to us that he is quite serious about it. He does indeed put on an antic disposition: he talks wildly, behaves oddly, is unpredictable, moody, and finally, dangerously violent. He does what his parents expect of him: nominated scapegoat, they expect him to become as delinquent as anyone could wish for.

This is the second important aspect of family scapegoating. It is a two-way system in which the scapegoat himself must co-operate fully in order to play the game by the family rules. Had Hamlet actively resisted, he could have thrown the system completely. If Rosencrantz, Guildenstern and Polonius, for example, had been met by an impressively composed and coherent

93

man every time they encountered Hamlet they would have been forced to think again: eventually, they would have had to go back to his parents and say, 'No, your son is definitely not insane, not that we can see: who is it here who's really crazy?' On the face of it, it may seem extraordinary that anyone should co-operate in accepting the role of scapegoat. But there are reasons for it. Family scapegoats are usually very dependent people – as Hamlet is. He is 30 years of age, exceptionally intelligent, courageous, attractive, and totally dependent on his family. He idolizes the image of a dead father (that image may have some good basis for reality in it) who is magnificently strong, wise and loving, 'an eye like Mars, the front of Jove' – a veritable god, who bears all the responsibility for his son. To take on anything of his father's mantle is the last thing Hamlet wants to do, and the very thought of responsibility in such a dependent personality makes him cringe with horror:

> O cursed spite,
> That ever I was born to set it right!

(p. 33)

So rather than be independent and take responsibility for setting the situation right, he remains in his dependent role and becomes the scapegoat. He gets a lot of attention this way, people want to look after him, do things for him, and he need never be held responsible for anything he does, however wild. Shakespeare gives Hamlet a short speech, towards the end of the play, which puts the whole issue nicely in a nutshell. Laertes understandably bears Hamlet some ill-will for having killed his father, Polonius. Hamlet tells him:

> This presence knows,
> And you must needs have heard, how I am punished
> With sore distraction. What I have done,
> That might your nature, honour and exception
> Roughly awake, I here proclaim was madness.
> Was't Hamlet wronged Laertes? Never Hamlet:
> If Hamlet from himself be ta'en away,
> And when he's not himself does wrong Laertes,
> Then Hamlet does it not; Hamlet denies it.
> Who does it then? His madness.

(p. 131)

By being able to fall back on his so-called madness, Hamlet can deny responsibility for virtually anything he does whenever it suits him. This is a considerable advantage to have in life, and one that many of us might envy at times of crisis.* But not many of us would be prepared to pay the same heavy price for being able to escape from his own responsibility to be scapegoat, and to suffer the pain of his parents' problems for them. And certainly he does suffer extreme agonies of guilt on behalf of Gertrude and Claudius. He worries incessantly about the murder of his father, almost as if he has done the deed himself. Claudius, the real villain, spares very little thought for the crime, and, as for Gertrude, she never thinks of it once. Hamlet is again tormented by his mother's sexual guilt – her betrayal of her dead husband, her blind, indiscriminate sexual appetite – while she herself has no trouble at all in locking up her conscience in who knows what hidden recesses of her mind. As he says,

> . . . O, most wicked speed, to post
> With such dexterity to incestous sheets!

(p. 14)

This of course is what being a scapegoat is all about – the specially elected goat which suffered for the sins of the whole tribe.

Being a scapegoat, Hamlet also gives another quality to the family interaction. He gives his mother and stepfather a relationship which otherwise they could not have. The major event which has brought Claudius and Gertrude together – the death of Hamlet Senior – is for them a taboo subject. By their own rules they are not allowed to discuss the most important mutual problem

---

* There is another way of interpreting Hamlet's use of his madness to excuse his murder of Polonius. At the time that Shakespeare was writing the medieval Catholic concept of the 'state of grace' was still an important part of everyday life. Thus, the killing whilst mad is an action carried out at a time when the murderer is temporarily out of this state of grace – and thus his action is potentially forgivable, it is possible for him to return to the state of grace. As a good Christian (Catholic?), Hamlet here lives up to man's hardest task – to fuse justice and grace in an almost decisive way. We know that he had made up his mind to murder Claudius: what we can understand, using this argument, is that both Hamlet's and Claudius' past and future acts are forgivable, in that it is their madness that speaks when they become involved in acts of murder. (Acknowledgment to Danish psychologist Kurt Palsvig for this illuminating insight.)

95

in their lives. This leaves them a great deal of unexpressed anxiety and very little conversation, or would have done save for the convenient occurrence of Hamlet's madness. Hamlet becomes their conversation-piece, their topic for communication with each other which would otherwise be no communication at all:

> QUEEN   Ah, mine own Lord, what have I seen tonight!
> KING   What, Gertrude? How does Hamlet?
> QUEEN   Mad as the sea and wind, when both contend. . . .
>
> (p. 90)

As we can see from the above, it is vital for the royal family to maintain a scapegoat, and likewise the scapegoat needs to be placed in that special role. This gives him status, a kind of perverted love and affection, and everyone is satisfied – even after a while Hamlet himself.

Secrets and their effect upon the family
(see also chapter 4)

Secrets in the family are usually what you might call 'open' secrets. That is, everyone in the family knows or partly knows what this or that secret is all about, and at the same time that knowledge continues to be guarded with the same fearful and fanatical caution that the major nations might accord to their most secret war weapon. Most major nations worth their salt know each other's secrets backwards anyway, and their elaborate and expensive security arrangements serve no better purpose than to maintain a large number of bureaucrats safely in employment and keep the feverish imaginations of thriller-writers busy and productive. Meanwhile the obstinate preservation of secrets does not help greatly to foster a feeling of mutual trust between different individuals in the environment of the family.

The fact is, every family has secrets. It is one thing to keep the secrets away from friends and relatives, it is quite another thing to try to hide the secrets from the children. Most of the families the authors have worked with have noted sooner or later that the children knew the secrets all the time. One of the authors worked with a family where the mother had been seduced by her father. This was her terrible secret. She insisted on telling me privately.

Equally I insisted that in addition to telling me about it she should also mention it in the family session. She agreed to do this with fear and trepidation. As I suspected, the children knew all about it. They said, 'Oh, that. We knew about that a long time ago. We heard you talk about it one night to Aunt Mary.'

Hamlet's feeling of natural distrust, regarding his mother and stepfather and their 'o'er hasty marriage' is inflated to gigantic proportions by the secrecy surrounding his father's death.

> O most pernicious woman!
> O villain, villain: smiling, damnéd villain!
>
> (p. 30)

Those secrets breed more secrets, which destroy trust.

His father's murder is the principal secret in Hamlet's family. Hamlet himself knows all the details of the crime from the end of Act I onwards; but despite this his parents continue to insist throughout the play that he does not know anything about it at all. He gives them two very clear messages indicating his full awareness of the secret – the first in the 'Mouse-Trap' play which is presented ostensibly for court entertainment, the second in his private confrontation with his mother in her bedroom. The play which Hamlet puts on is a macabre and spectacular piece of stagecraft, in which the exact circumstances of his father's poisoning and his mother's swift marriage to the assassin are re-enacted, first in mime and then in dialogue by the players in his cunning little melodrama. The play is Hamlet's method of communicating a two-fold message to his parents, who are for the short span his captive audience: first, that he knows all about the conspiracy behind Hamlet Senior's death, and second, that he wants to take the shroud of secrecy off the subject and bring it for open discussion in the family.

Now it is fair comment that this may be the most unorthodox and circuitous route ever taken by a son to communicate a straight message to his parents, and we have already talked about 'covert' communication in the Hamlet family. But the effect of this message is very plain to read from his parents watching the play, and the violence of the king's reaction is enough to leave no doubt that the message has come across to him loud and clear. He leaps from his seat, shouting for the play to be stopped, he disappears into his private chambers in an unexplained rage, and when he

97

next emerges on the stage his first words are to condemn Hamlet not only as insane but as an actual physical danger to life and property:

> I like him not; nor stands it safe with us
> To let his madness range. Therefore prepare you:
> I your commission will forthwith dispatch,
> And he to England shall along with you.
> The terms of our estate may not endure
> Hazard so dangerous as doth hourly grow
> Out of his lunacies.
>
> (p. 79)

Hamlet, by his albeit roundabout efforts to bring the family secrets out into the open, has committed the most serious outrage possible. He has threatened the private, closeted guilt of his parents, who will see their son dead first rather than have to take the wraps off the family secret. The secret is so precious, so deadly, that the King will employ:

> Our sovereign process, which imports at full
> By letters congruing to that effect,
> The present death of Hamlet. Do it, England;
> For like the hectic in my blood he rages
> And thou must cure me.
>
> (p. 95)

It is of course the terrible anxiety of his parents' guilty secret that rages so fervently in their blood; and Hamlet's behaviour is only seen by them as 'a hazard so near us' because it threatens their secret with possible exposure. At all costs the secret must be protected, at the expense of life itself, and with a deadly earnestness that exceeds the bounds of all possible logic or justification.

Claudius and Gertrude try to protect their secret by counter-accusing their son of having secrets. Hamlet, unhappily for them, has no real secrets to hide, but that does not prevent his determined parents from attributing to him secrets which he does not possess. They ask him, right at the start of the play, why he is upset, and when he tells them in as many words they simply refuse to hear it and they press ahead with the assumption that there must be some other ulterior motive behind his gloom and despondency. So they send messengers to spy on him, to engage him in conversation, and to accuse him by implication of keeping a secret which he is too guilty to reveal. The psychiatric term for this kind of behaviour is 'projection': a neurotic with his back against the wall will defend himself by seeing his own short-comings in other people, and will accuse them as bitterly and in-dignantly as any martyred innocent. The King and Queen are certainly projecting onto Hamlet in this issue of secrecy, for at any stage they could have called on their son and received a direct answer to the direct question:

> Why he puts on this confusion,
> Grating so harshly all his days of quiet
> With turbulent and dangerous lunacy?
>
> (p. 58)

Similarly all their efforts to find out what is happening to his relationship with Ophelia: their elaborate schemes of eaves-dropping are really quite unnecessary, when all they need have done was to ask Hamlet their question outright. But they choose not to do this. They have a vested interest in promoting secrecy in their son, because of their own guilty commitment to the pro-tection that secrecy affords. They go to these extreme lengths to cast their son's openness and honesty in doubt, so that finally they can have the tremendous satisfaction of hearing it said of him:

> Nor do we find him forward to be sounded;
> But, with a crafty madness, keeps aloof
> When we would bring him on to some confession
> Of his true state.
>
> (p. 58)

This speech comes from Guildenstern, who in theory should not be involved in the family round of secrecy. Guildenstern, Rosen-crantz and Polonius are three individuals outside the play of the Hamlet nuclear family. Somehow, against what slight evidence of impartial judgment they show, they have become caught in the web of the family conspiracy. Like the three wise monkeys, they will neither hear, see nor speak any evil against the King and Queen.

These three demonstrate some of the interesting side effects of secrecy which overspill the nuclear family into the extended family and beyond. They are all three used as pawns in the game

99

whose main object is to preserve the *status quo* of secrecy in the royal family. Rosencrantz and Guildenstern allow this to happen partly because of their ignorance and inexperience of the family background, and partly because their perception is overshadowed by their awe of the King and Queen's authority. Polonius should suffer from neither of these defects: he has been around long enough to know the family as intimately as anyone, and in his official capacity as Lord Chamberlain has enough authority of his own to release him from any false awe of the throne. But he is none the less very anxious about his position in court. He is like a man who holds high office in a company more through his personal friendship with the boss than his own competence in the job: suddenly the boss is dead, and the company has a new director who is not quite as approachable or friendly as his predecessor. Polonius is in a panic: will the new king be as tolerant of his incompetence as Hamlet Senior was? His main concern is therefore to impress Claudius, and one suggestion from the King that Hamlet is supposedly keeping secrets is enough to send Polonius scampering off on the most bizarre spying adventures. Since Polonius has a fetish of his own with secrecy and spying, this frantic chase after non-existent secrets fulfills a personal need in him.

The two most striking aspects of Polonius' character are, first, his obsession with other people's secrets, and second, his own private anxiety, never openly expressing it but referring to it constantly by his behaviour, his babbling, meaningless conversation, his ceaseless activity, and his portly trundlings from one keyhole to another. One can imagine his eye taking on a keyhole shape with the evolution of too much practice, and his ear bent permanently to an angle most suitable for slipping into cracks in doorways. His whole life seems to be directed to no other end but to keep himself permanently occupied and his mind away from other things.

Now the reasons for this special anxiety of his are open to some conjecture. He is anxious, obviously, about his job as Lord Chamberlain. But perhaps he also has some deeper, more acute anxiety relating to the very same secret which dogs the rest of the family – the circumstances of Hamlet Senior's death. It is not beyond the bounds of possibility that, somewhere in the twilight regions of his mind, he might have half known, half guessed, at something approaching a suspicion of foul play. A man like Polonius would have recoiled from that suspicion with terror and dismay; but it would stay with him no matter how hard he tried to push it away, lurking at the edge of his consciousness. And he deals with the anxiety that this causes in the same way that Gertrude and Claudius deal with it – by projecting it onto other people. The real secret is suppressed, and Polonius finds himself a convenient preoccupation with substitute secrets – the non-existent secrets of his son Laertes, his daughter Ophelia, and Hamlet.

When he dies ignominiously on the end of Hamlet's rapier, Polonius dies the victim of his own compulsive curiosity. But more than that, he dies a victim of the family secret, a conspiracy of silence which has drawn him in and dealt him early and une-expected death. He is the first casualty on a death list which by the end of the play will total eight people, all similarly victims of the same conspiracy. The play itself is a legend for its heavy casualties – in one early performance the stage boards collapsed under the weight of falling bodies in the last scene. Moral messages are distinctly not a characteristic of Shakespeare's plays, but in *Hamlet* the sound of those falling bodies must serve as a comment on the consequences of obsessive secrecy in the family.

Notes

1 We are grateful to Mr Paul Kastning for calling this to our attention, and for the translation.
2 *Family Life*, directed by Ken Loach, distributed by Kestrel Films.

3 THE TYRONE FAMILY

Long Day's Journey into Night by Eugene O'Neill

List of characters

James Tyrone	Father
Mary Cavan Tyrone	Mother
James Tyrone, Jr	Eldest Son
Edmund Tyrone	Youngest Son
Kathleen Tyrone	Second Girl

> I've tried to make allowances. Christ, you have to make
> allowances in this damn family or go nuts! I have tried to
> make allowances for myself when I remember all the rotten
> stuff I have pulled!

Synopsis of the plot of the play

The first act takes place in the living room of the Tyrones'
summer home, shortly after breakfast. Very quickly we are precipitated into a family that is torn by conflict and argument.
Edmund, we learn, is ill and there is a secret connected with the
mother of which everyone seems afraid.

In the second act which is set before and after lunch on this
same day, we learn that the mother's secret is that she is a drug
addict. For some time the men had believed that she might be
cured, but it now becomes obvious that she has started again. We
also learn that Edmund has consumption, and that he plans to
visit the doctor that same afternoon. The thought that Edmund is
sick obviously terrifies Mary, and there is a kind of conspiracy to
keep her from thinking that it is anything serious.

The third act begins with Kathleen and Mary sharing the stage:

Mary is obviously very high on drugs – the two women had just returned from the village where they had bought Mary a fresh supply – and Kathleen is slowly becoming drunk. When Edmund and Tyrone arrive, Edmund tells his mother that he has consumption and will have to go into a sanatorium. She becomes angry and hysterical, not wanting to be told, not wanting to hear. In the end Edmund leaves the home, and Mary goes back to her room to get another injection, leaving Tyrone alone, angry and helpless.

In the final act late at night on the same day Edmund returns home, rather drunk, to find his father also rather drunk. The two of them talk and play cards until Jamie arrives when Tyrone runs out: not wanting to face the bitter tongue of his eldest son. There is a lot of anger and love and confession between the two brothers as there was between Edmund and his father. The play ends after Tyrone has come back in. The mother comes downstairs. She has fled into the past: the here and now no longer exists for her.

The closed family

The Tyrone family is locked by the twin emotions of fear and guilt. Together these two emotions strangle the obvious love the family members at times reveal. But for the Tyrones, even the revelation of their love has ultimately become a threat. Each member bears a cross that contributes to the family suffering: Tyrone is a miser, Mary a drug addict, Jamie a spendthrift alcoholic, and Edmund a drifter, and sick. They all have a need for love, but at the same time they all have a fear of love. The family stays together, but grows more angry and bitter. At the end of the play, we feel that the family has all but destroyed itself. The mother is almost psychotic, and has retreated to the past beyond her marriage, and Edmund is off to a sanatorium.

We devote the major part of this chapter to an analysis of the dynamics of a closed family. In the second and final sections we explore some of the alternatives by looking at the idea of growth.

The family as a closed system

The family as a system, for our purposes, has two parts – the behavioural and the communicative. The behavioural aspects of the family and those of the individual are culturally prescribed. For example, the majority of Danish middle-class familes are quite formal where outsiders are concerned. It is important for a Danish hostess, when inviting guests for dinner, to have plenty of time to prepare both the home and the meal in honour of the guest. It would be exceedingly rare for someone to be brought into the home to eat without such previous notice. The aim of the hostess is to creat a 'hyggelig' or 'cosy, snug' atmosphere.

We also find such highly defined expectations governing the family's interaction with the outside world in other countries. In France, for example, it may take a long time before a stranger is invited to visit with the family in a social way. The stranger must first establish a fairly good personal relationship with at least one member of the family.

Differences may vary in the same country from class to class. In England, for example, the working-class home tends to be a private place. Family members will meet with their friends there, but usually only as a preliminary to going out. The home is not a place to entertain. This can be very different from middle- and upper-class families where the home is seen as the natural place to entertain friends and colleagues (Goldthorp et al., 1971). It is very difficult to generalize in the case of America because of regional differences, but it would seem that in general there is an air of informality, and unexpected guests are cheerfully invited to take 'pot luck'.

The behavioural aspect to the family system, being culturally prescribed, can to some extent be viewed separately from the communication aspects. We wish to make it clear that the degree of openness or closedness that the family exhibits relative to the outside world is not necessarily a pathological symptom. The Danish family, which is very formal and appears closed, may communicate openly and honestly. Behaviour and communication are two variables which may operate independently of each other.

In this study we are particularly concerned with the communication aspects. We shall examine the concept of closedness along four major dimensions – agreement, honesty and spontaneity, difference, and limits of boundaries. (We are heavily indebted to Virginia Satir in this section. See Satir, 1967, pp. 185–6.) Probably the most extreme example of a closed family is the one where, at virtually all times, everyone is in agreement with everyone else (ibid., p. 185):

> The principal rule seems to be that everyone is supposed to have the same opinions, feelings, and desires, whether or not this is true. In closed systems, honest self-expression is impossible, and if it does occur, the expression is viewed as deviant or 'sick' or 'crazy' by the other members of the group or family. Differences are treated as dangerous.

In such families, disagreements are too anxiety-provoking to be acceptable. Such anxiety can be based on either fantasy or reality. The actual fear has been learned from somewhere, usually from parental figures. These patterns have often developed from generation to generation and are extremely difficult to break. Laing (1971, p. 24), when speaking of a case of his, says:

> We can just glimpse in this family a drama perpetuated over three generations – the players are two women and a man: First, mother, daughter, and father; Second, mother, daughter, and daughter's son. Daughter's father dies – daughter conceives a son *to replace* [italics original] her father. The play is the thing. The actors come and go. As they die, others are born. The new-born enters the part vacated by the newly-dead. The system perpetuates itself over generations; the young are introduced to the parts that the dead once played. Hence, the drama continues. The dramatic structure abides, subject to transformations whose laws we have not yet formulated and whose existence we have barely begun to fathom.

An exquisite example of a closed family can be found at the beginning of T. S. Eliot's *The Family Reunion*. Briefly, the scene is set at Wishwood, an upper middle-class country home. It is the mother's birthday and all the family are to gather together – including aunts, uncles, brothers and sisters. The highlight of the reunion is to be the return of Harry, the eldest and favourite son. He has been away from home for eight years, having made a marriage which his mother disapproved of. However, shortly before the play opens, the wife has drowned at sea, which is the reason for Harry's return at this time. Whilst waiting for him to arrive, the family is anticipating him by discussing what it will be like:

AGATHA   It is going to be rather painful for Harry,
             After eight years and all that has happened,
             To come back to Wishwood.
GERALD   Why, painful?
VIOLET   Gerald! You know what Agatha means.
AGATHA   I mean painful, because everything is irrevocable –
             Because the past is irremediable,
             Because the future can only be built
             Upon the real past. Wandering in the tropics
             Or against the painted sea of the Mediterranean,
             Harry must often have remembered Wishwood –
             The nursery tea, the school holiday,
             The daring feats on the old pony,
             And thought to creep back through the little door.
             He will find a new Wishwood. Adaptation is hard.
AMY   Nothing has changed, Agatha, at Wishwood.
             Everything is kept as it was when he left it,
             Except the old pony, and the mongrel setter
             Which I had to have destroyed.
             Nothing has been changed. I have seen to that.

                                      (pp. 16–17)

We can describe what is happening here in the language of family therapy. If we analyse that final speech that Amy made in this way, what does it reveal?

'Nothing has changed, Agatha, at Wishwood.'
Change is dangerous, we don't want it here.
'Everything is kept as it was when he left it.'
Everything is going to be really nice, just like it used to be.
'Except the old pony and the mongrel setter which I had to have destroyed.'
Some things are beyond even my control, I'm sorry to say.
'Nothing has been changed. I have seen to that.'
I'm just going to win this game.

The long-awaited favourite son enters the room. He is having hallucinations:

HARRY   Look there, look there:
          Do you see them?
GERALD   No I don't see anyone about.
HARRY   No, no, not there. Look there!
          Can't you see them? *You* don't see them, but I see
            them,
          And they see me. This is the first time that I have
            seen them.
          In the Java Straits, in the Sunda Sea,
          In the sweet sickly tropical night, I knew they were
            coming.
          In Italy, from behind the nightingale's thicket,
          The eyes stared at me, and corrupted that song.
          Behind the palm trees in the Grand Hotel,
          They were always there. But I did not *see* them.
          Why should they wait until I come back to
            Wishwood?
          There were a thousand places where I might have
            met them!
          Why here? Why here?
          Many happy returns of the day mother,
          Aunt Ivy, Aunt Violet, Uncle Gerald,
          Uncle Charles, Agatha.
AMY   We are very glad to have you back, Harry.
          Now we shall be all together for dinner.

                                  (pp. 23–4)

This is a total denial, the kind of thing one often sees in a closed family. Moreover, the family hastened to preserve the illusion that nothing whatsoever had changed in the past eight years:

AMY   We are very glad to have you back Harry,
          Now we shall all be together for dinner.
          The servants have been looking forward to your
            coming:
          Would you like to have them in after dinner
          Or wait until tomorrow? I am sure you must be
            tired.
          You'll find everybody here, and everything the
            same.

Mr Bevon – you remember – wants to call
  tomorrow
On some legal business, a question about taxes –
But I think you would rather wait until you are
  rested.
Your room is all ready for you. Nothing has been
  changed.

HARRY   Changed, Nothing changed? How can you say that
  nothing has changed?
You all look so withered and young.

GERALD   We must have a ride tomorrow.
You'll find you know the country as well as ever
There wasn't an inch of it you didn't know.
But you will have to see about a couple of new
  hunters.

CHARLES   And I've a new wine merchant to recommend to
  you;
Your cellar could do with a little attention.

IVY   And you really have to find a successor to old
  Hawkins.
It's really high-time the old man was pensioned.
He's let the rock garden go to rack and ruin.
And he's nearly half blind. I've spoken to your
  mother
Time and time again: She's done nothing about it
Because she preferred to wait for your coming.

VIOLET   And time and time again I have spoken to your
  mother
About the waste that goes on in the kitchen.
Mrs Packell is too old to know what she is doing.
It really needs a man in charge of things at
  Wishwood.

AMY   You see your Aunts and Uncles are very helpful,
  Harry.
I have always found them forthcoming with advice
Which I have never taken. Now it is your business.
I have struggled to keep Wishwood going
And to make no changes before your return.
Now it is for you to manage. I am an old woman.
They can give me no further advice when I am dead.

IVY   Oh, dear Amy!
No one wants you to die, I'm sure!
Now that Harry is back, is the time to think of living.

HARRY   Time and time and time, and change, no change!
All of you try to talk as if nothing had happened
And yet you are talking of nothing else. Why not
    get to the point?
Or if you want to pretend that I am another
    person –
A person who you have conspired to invent, please
    do so
In my absence. I shall be less embarrassing to you,
    Agatha.

(p. 24–6)

Such a closed family will go to enormous lengths to maintain
the illusion of permanency, even to the extent of denying reality.
With Harry's family, ultimately his only course of action, if he is
to maintain his own integrity, is to run away from them.

The use of agreement to keep the family closed can take many
forms. In Eliot's family every attempt is made to make it total.
Another way in which it is used is in the 'rubber ball' syndrome,
where the child continuingly agrees with everyone else, even
though they disagree. By this means open dissension is avoided,
and everyone apparently has an ally, and a source of affection.
The Tyrone family demonstrate yet a third way in which agreement can be used.

Every family has its sensitive areas. One way the family could
handle this is to have a system of rules. This has two functions.
It provides for safety and the avoidance of pain by delineating
when, in what way, and with whom such issues can be talked
about. In the Tyrone family there is such a sensitive area associated
with every person. With Jamie it is his alcoholism; with Edmund
his illness; the mother is a drug addict; the father a miser. Under
certain circumstances, each of these areas can become a forbidden
topic. For example, the men together can talk about Edmund's
consumption, but must not even mention it when the mother is
present. Such agreements are forged by fear of pain. There is a
rule in the Tyrone family – you must not make anyone suffer
unless they allow it.

Jamie and Tyrone are discussing the mother:

TYRONE (*sadly*) I know. (*Tensely.*) Well, what was it? Can't
you speak out?

JAMIE Nothing, I tell you. Just my damned foolishness.
Around three o'clock this morning I woke up and heard
her moving around in the spare room. Then she went to
the bathroom. I pretended to be asleep. She stopped in the
hall to listen, as if she wanted to make sure I was.

TYRONE (*forced scorn*) For God's sake, is that all? She told me
herself the fog horn kept her awake all night, and every
night since Edmund's been sick, she has been up and down,
going to his room to see how he was.

JAMIE (*eagerly*) Yes, that's right, she did stop to listen outside
his room. (*Hesitatingly again.*) It was her being in the spare
room that scared me. I couldn't help remembering that
when she starts sleeping alone in there, it has always been
a sign –

TYRONE It isn't this time! It's easily explained. Where else
could she go last night to get away from my snoring? (*He
gives way to a burst of resentful anger.*) By God, how you
can live with a mind that sees nothing but the worst
motives behind everything is beyond me!

JAMIE (*stung*) Don't pull that! I've just said that I was all
wrong. Don't you suppose that I am as glad of that as you are!

TYRONE (*mollifyingly*) I'm sure you are Jamie. (*A pause. His
expression becomes sombre. He speaks slowly with a
superstitious dread.*) It would be like a curse she can't
escape if worry over Edmund – it was in her long sickness
after bringing him into the world that she first –

JAMIE She didn't have anything to do with it!

TYRONE I'm not blaming her.

JAMIE (*bitingly*) Then who are you blaming? Edmund for
being born?

TYRONE You damn fool! No one was to blame.

JAMIE The bastard of a doctor was! From what Momma
said, he was another cheap quack like Hardy! You wouldn't
pay for a first-rate –

TYRONE That's a lie! (*Furiously.*) So I am to blame! That's
what you are driving at, is it? You evil-minded loafer!

JAMIE   Shhh! (*Warningly as he hears his mother in the dining room.*) Shhh!

(*Tyrone gets hastily to his feet and goes to look out of the windows at right. Jamie speaks with complete change of tone.*)

Well, if we are going to cut the front hedge today, we had better go to work.

(PP. 33-4)

In this example father and son display their secret fear – later to be amply justified – concerning Mary. When she enters the room they stop instantly any reference to her, and in doing so reveal their fear and their embarrassment.

Agreements are made between individuals not to talk about certain subjects which are taboo. If such areas are violated, one member will signal to the other, verbally or non-verbally, that he is suffering. This acts as a distress signal, and the violator will back off, usually making some effort to help the other person's pain. Tyrone breaks such a rule by talking to Mary about her addiction:

TYRONE (*with guilty resentment*)   For God's sake, don't dig up what's long forgotten. If you are that far gone in the past already, when it is only the beginning of the afternoon, what will you be tonight?

MARY (*stares at him defiantly now*)   Come to think of it, I do have to drive up-town. There is something I must get at the drug store.

TYRONE (*bitterly scornful*)   Leave it to you to have some of the stuff hidden, and prescriptions for more! I hope you lay in a good stock ahead so we will never have another night like the one where you screamed for it, and ran out of the house in your night-dress half-crazy, to try to throw yourself off the dock!

MARY (*tries to ignore this*)   I have to get tooth powder and toilet soap and cold cream – (*She breaks down pitiably.*) James, you mustn't remember! You mustn't humiliate me so!

TYRONE (*ashamed*)   I'm sorry. Forgive me, Mary!

MARY (*defensively detached*)   It doesn't matter. Nothing like that ever happened. You must have dreamed it.

(*He stares at her hopelessly. Her voice seems to drift farther and farther away.*)

I was so healthy before Edmund was born. You remember, James. There wasn't a nerve in my body. Even travelling with you season after season, with week after week of one-night stands, in trains without Pullmans, in dirty rooms of filthy hotels, eating bad food, bearing children in hotel rooms, I still kept healthy. But bearing Edmund was the last straw. I was so sick afterwards, and that ignorant quack of a cheap hotel doctor – ALL he knew was that I was in pain. It was easy for him to stop the pain.

TYRONE   Mary! For God's sake, forget the past!

(pp. 74–5)

Here we see Mary's ambivalence about her own addiction. But eventually she completely denies it, and in doing so forces Tyrone to agree with her. She does this by first of all letting him know that he is hurting her, and then by blackmailing him, insinuating that he is responsible for her present position.

Areas like this become forbidden because they are so sensitive. However, in the Tyrone family, there are so many of these areas that the relationships are seeded with emotional land-mines. This leaves little room for honesty or spontaneity. What spontaneity there is among the Tyrones continually gets them into trouble. By acting without thinking, the members are continually stepping onto the land-mines, and the relationships keep exploding. In the final act, in a discussion between Tyrone and Edmund, we can list nine denials which all result as the consequences of one or the other mentioning a forbidden topic. Here we will take a brief sequence to exemplify the point:

TYRONE (*Keeps shuffling the cards fumblingly, forgetting to deal them*)   As I was saying, you must take her tales of the past with a grain of salt. The piano playing and her dream of becoming a concert pianist. That was put in her head by the Nuns flattering her. She was their pet. They loved her for being so devout. They're innocent women anyway, when it comes to the world. They don't know that not one in a million who shows promise ever rises to concert playing. Not that your mother didn't play well for a schoolgirl, but that is no reason to take it for granted that she could have –

EDMUND (*sharply*) Why don't you deal, if we are going to
play.

TYRONE Eh? I am. (*Dealing with very uncertain judgment of
distance*.) And the idea that she might have become a Nun.
That's the worst. Your mother was one of the most
beautiful girls you could ever see. She knew it too. She was
a bit of a rogue and a coquette, God bless her, behind all
her shyness and blushes. She was never made to renounce
the world. She was bursting with health and high spirits
and the love of living.

EDMUND For God's sake, Poppa! Why don't you pick up
your hand?

TYRONE (*picks it up – dully*) Yes, let's see what I have here.
(*They both stare at their cards unseeingly. Then they both start.
Tyrone whispers*.)
Listen!

EDMUND She's coming downstairs.

TYRONE (*hurriedly*) We'll play our game. Pretend not to
notice and she will soon go up again.

EDMUND (*staring through the front parlour – with relief*) I don't
see her. She must have started down and then turned back.

TYRONE Thank God.

(pp. 119–20)

In the above quotation there are three examples of denial, two
by Edmund, one by Tyrone. This pattern permeates all the communication in the Tyrone family. Everyone is encompassed in a
'blame frame'. When this happens, people usually get labelled,
and this in turn leads to growth being restricted. The blame frame
in the Tyrone family leads to labels like 'drunk', 'crazy', 'miser',
'dope fiend', etc. In this way any communication which poses a
disturbance or threat is immediately blocked and the person
temporarily discredited. When communication is blocked in this
way, the individual is forced to rescind his feelings, and internalize
them. The more areas closed in this way, the less possibilities
there are for sharing and learning. Eventually, the person may
become immobilized. In this situation, what are the person's
alternatives? He can stay with the family and go on suffering;
or he can leave his family and seek relationships elsewhere. The
important thing to remember is that a closed system rarely is able

113

to change itself without the help of an outside influence (see figure 1).

The blame frame is one of the many strategies used by families' members to maintain the closed system. Figure 1 lists the ways in which people attempt to survive when they feel themselves threatened. The threat itself may be actual or it may exist only in

Perceived threats to survival

Blocking	Ignore what is happening: pretend that you haven't heard. Leave the scene. Selective inattention. Misinterpretation. Joking. Sleep. Alcoholism. Drugs.
Discrediting	Joking. Bringing in irrelevant material. Discrediting the others' motivation. Humiliation. Labelling. Sarcasm. Agreement.
Blame	Rejection. Assault. Mental illness. Murder. Suicide.

Individual

Figure 1   Strategies for survival

the persons' fantasy. When fantasies distort responses in family relationships in this way at bottom there is often a basic fear, 'will the family survive if this is allowed to continue?' (See section on 'Survival', p. 195.)

For the purposes of elucidation we can take one item from each category and examine it within the closed family system. Leaving the scene is a very good way of blocking. It terminates communication and leaves the other person completely frustrated, for there is very little that he can do. It can have a very special meaning when applied to younger children. Unlike adults, their ability physically to leave the situation is very limited. One very effective way of 'leaving' the other person is to withdraw completely into self. This we label autism.

Joking, when used to discredit, is a very special ploy, and can be extremely effective. It can have two effects: it humiliates the recipient of the humour without allowing him any legitimate manoeuvre to retaliate. We have joking in both the first and second categories, for it can also be used to block communication.

By committing suicide, the individual is saying that his life is no longer bearable. At the same time he is maybe blaming his family, and this is the way he may make them feel guilty for what he believes they have done to him.

Up to this point we have been discussing the structure of the closed family system. Now we would like to concentrate on two major types of communication – overt and confused – that can take place within such a system.

The qualities which mark overt communication are honesty and accuracy. In a healthy family, it is used by the members to share and to help. But the same style of communication, when used in a closed family system, such as the Tyrones', is used to control and to wound. In the final act, the two brothers come together late at night and talk. They discuss the whole family, including themselves. At times they seek deliberately to hurt each other:

> JAMIE (*confusedly – appearing drunk again*)   Don't be a dumb-bell! What I said . . . Always suspected of hoping for the worst. I've got so I can't help – (*Then drunkenly resentful.*) What are you trying to do, accuse me? Don't play the wise guy with me! I've learnt more of life than you will ever know! Just because you have read a lot of high-brow junk, don't think you can fool me! You're only an overgrown kid! Momma's baby and Poppa's pet! The family White Hope! You've been getting a swelled head lately. About nothing! About a few poems in a hick town newspaper! Hell, I used to write better stuff for the Lit. magazine in College! You'd better wake up! You're setting no rivers on fire! You let hick town boobs flatter you with bunk about your future –
>
> (pp. 143–4)

At one point the feelings are so violent that the assault becomes physical:

> JAMIE (*quoting a poem*)   If I were hanged on the highest hill,
>   Mother o' mine O Mother o' mine!
>   I know whose love would follow me
>   still . . .

EDMUND (*violently*)   Shut up!

JAMIE (*in a cruel, sneering tone with hatred in it*)   Where's the hop-head? Gone to sleep?

(*Edmund jerks as if he had been struck. There is a tense silence. Edmund's face looks stricken and sick. Then in a burst of rage, he springs from his chair.*)

EDMUND   You dirty bastard!

(*He punches his brother in the face, a blow that glances off the cheek bone. For a second Jamie reacts pugnaciously and half-rises from his chair to do battle, but suddenly he seems to sober up to a shock realization of what he has said and he sinks back limply.*)

(p. 142)

The Tyrone family is fairly unsophisticated when it comes to handling its feelings. Although verbally they could be very sophisticated, it is obvious that when it comes to talking about themselves within the family they are pretty hopeless. Within the framework of the closed family system, one of the likely results of being so unsophisticated may be a pattern of anger and violence.

Every family needs love to survive. Each family has its own special ways of demonstrating love and affection – even the Tyrones. As the play opens, Tyrone and Mary enter the living room:

TYRONE   You're a fine armful now, Mary, with those twenty pounds you've gained.

MARY (*smiles affectionately*)   I've gotten too fat, you mean, dear. I really ought to reduce.

TYRONE   None of that, my Lady! You're just right. We'll have no talk of reducing. Is that why you ate so little breakfast?

MARY   So little? I thought I ate a lot.

TYRONE   You didn't. Not as much as I would like to see anyway.

MARY (*teasingly*)   Oh you! You expect everyone to eat the enormous breakfast you do. No one else in the world could do so without dying of indigestion.

(*She comes forward to stand by the right of the table.*)

TYRONE (*following her*)   I hope I am not as big a glutton as
   that sounds. (*With hearty satisfaction.*) But thank God, I've
   kept my appetite and have a digestion of a young man of
   twenty, if I am sixty-five.
MARY   You surely have, James. No one could deny that.

(p. 12)

This is in fact our first view of the Tyrone family and it looks
as if the family expresses affection easily. But this is not the case.
The pattern that we discover reveals that openly shown affection
is somehow threatening, because it is always very quickly inter-
rupted in some way. Just a few minutes after the above conversation, we have an example:

MARY   What makes you think I am upset?
TYRONE   Why nothing, except you've seemed a bit high-
   strung the past few days.
MARY (*forcing a smile*)   I have? Nonsense, dear. It's your
   imagination. (*With sudden tenseness.*) You really must not
   watch me all the time, James. I mean, it makes me self-
   conscious.
TYRONE (*putting a hand over one of her nervously playing ones*)
   Now, now, Mary. That's your imagination. If I have
   watched you, it was to admire how fat and beautiful you
   looked. (*His voice is suddenly moved by deep feelings.*) I can't
   tell you the deep happiness it gives me, darling, to see you
   as you've been since you came back to us, your dear old
   self again. (*He leans over and kisses her cheek impulsively –
   then turning back, adds with a constrained air.*) So keep up
   the good work, Mary.
MARY (*has turned her head away*)   I will, dear. (*She gets up
   restlessly and goes to the windows at right.*) Thank heavens
   the fog is gone. (*She turns back.*) I do feel out of sorts this
   morning. I wasn't able to get much sleep with that awful
   fog horn going all night long.

(p. 14)

Here, Mary handles the affection by changing the subject. At
other times, various other ways are used – arguments are picked,
or pain is inflicted. This formula is used for all emotions within
the closed family system of the Tyrones. Anger may lead to

117

violence, affection may lead to love. Both results could be dangerous for the family members, and so must be avoided. It is the
survival of the family which is at stake. To accept love would
mean that all the pain had to be shared openly and honestly. To
precipitate violence could mean the end of the family.

In looking at the Tyrone family, we are forced to wonder what
keeps them together. The conflicts are great, and they seem to
demonstrate a minimum amount of affection. But the family
members do have positive feelings for each other. As we have
seen, they are able to state in a very low-key term how they feel –
though seldom clearly. When this happens in closed family
systems, it leads to confused communication. This is because the
emotions are so potentially dangerous, they must be disguised or
mixed in with other information.

Confused communication represents a bid to remain safe. The
actor is saying that he is in pain and that he wants contact. He is
saying: 'I would like to if I could. But I am too scared. Something
terrible might happen to me. I might be destroyed.' At the same
time, he is asking for help. His confusion is a kind of distress
signal. This method of communicating can present great problems
for the recipient. It must be remembered, however, that in a
closed family system the recipient is likely to have been involved
himself in such a communication pattern, possibly from the very
beginning. Family theory tends to indicate that such patterns are
learned from parents.

The child raised in a family where confusion is the principal
characteristic of its communication, is highly unlikely to be given
the opportunity to develop adequate skills to make constructive
relationships in the outside world. He is likely to have low self-
esteem, not trust anyone, lack stable values, does not trust himself
to be open, and will be terrified by the idea of commitment. With
these deficiencies, he will be unable to formulate what it is that he
wants.

In the closed family, everyone is responsible for the patterns of
communication which develop, and each individual person will
display, in varying degrees, the characteristics of confused communication. In this way such a family will perpetuate itself, and
become tightly locked in its patterns. The individual, ill-equipped
to cope with the outside world, will often remain with the family,
because there at least, he feels a certain degree of safety, and

receives a certain amount of affection. There are other alternatives, but because of the bind that he feels he is in, most of them will probably be retreatist or self-destructive. For example, alcoholism, drug addiction, prostitution, or criminality. A fifth major escape route is into the world of the mental patient. We would like to examine this last alternative in some depth as it is highly germane to the theory of family therapy.

There has been an extensive amount of literature produced on the mental hospital, and the etiology of mental illness. This has been done both by professionals and patients. What we would like to do is add another dimension, drawing heavily from the works of Szasz, Scheff, Goffman, Satir, Cooper and Laing.

It is our thesis that the mental hospital is sometimes perceived as being a desirable alternative for some individuals to the chaotic pressures of their family and our society. Further, that the family, the courts, and even the hospitals, may become co-conspirators in labelling the person as being 'mad'.

Figure 2 represents the complete process in a simplified form

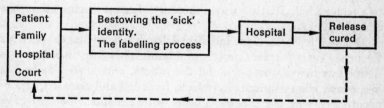

Figure 2

beginning with the conspiracy and sometimes ending with discharge from hospital, although the dotted line is there to show that it can, in fact, become a circular process.

The conspiracy is spread out over a period of time, beginning in the family. Here, at some point, a change occurs which is defined as bad or unacceptable. Usually it will involve one individual beginning to act in a 'strange' way. The rest of the family gets scared, and feel they cannot tolerate what is happening. Unless there is a return to normality rather quickly, a crisis develops. If this occurs, the next step is usually to call in a professional – someone whom the family perceives as being an outside expert.

This marks the beginning of the labelling process and the conspiracy is under way: usually the family has already defined the problem, and they call in the expert to validate their opinion and to do something about it. Laing describes this process (1971, p. 24):

> When I have been called into a situation, usually one person has come to be regarded as having 'something the matter with' him or her; usually, 'expert' opinion has also begun to see something 'mentally' the matter with this one person.

If at this point the outside expert and the family agree on defining the individual as sick, a number of things start to happen. (Goffman (1970, p. 126) describes this process as involving what he calls 'a circuit of agents'.) Broadly speaking, two possible paths can be followed. The first climaxes in voluntary commitment for the individual to the mental hospital. This presupposes that he will not object too strongly to what is happening to him. If he does, then there is a second possibility. This will involve the use of legal sanction so that the person gets committed by court order to the hospital. In this way the courts become involved in the conspiracy.

Meanwhile, what of the individual? He has been blamed perhaps for many years for the family's problems. This latest incident was defined as being worse than all the others, and proved to be the last straw. His symptoms have been recorded and assessed, and in accordance with the diagnosis he is to be certified. He may have been through the indignity of a court appearance, by which his freedom is taken from him by the State.

We have stated that the individual is part of the conspiracy. What exactly does he gain? We must see it in terms of him leaving one world, the family, and entering another, the hospital. The two worlds are very, very different. It is almost like going from a land of chaos to a land of order. The immediate gains are twofold: separation from family and freedom from responsibility. There are other subsidiary gains, however. The new patient will become a part of a smooth-running organization whose sole aim is to take care of him. He will be given a schedule, which will include all things like feeding time, bed time, visiting time, candy time, bath time, work time, fun time, medicine time, and treatment time. When we compare all this to his life in the family and the world outside, these gains can be more clearly seen. He may very well have been bullied, harassed and humiliated by his family, whilst finding it more and more difficult to function at work or socially. Given these two contrasts, entering hospital could prove to be a great relief. Thus the actual process of entering hospital assumes a special importance.

In Goffman's classic analysis of total institutions (*Asylums*, 1970), he describes in some detail the admission procedure. This admission procedure marks the boundary between two lives. It must almost be said that the individual assumes a new role by passing through this procedure.

Like the monastery, the hospital acts like a retreat from the world. However, in secular terms, it is a big business. There are few businesses that want to go bankrupt, and hospitals are no exception. The aim is to keep their beds full. And, like every other good business, they do not wish to lose a single customer. Hospital staff are likely to become anxious when they see empty beds. Here is the motivation for their part in the conspiracy. A vignette captures this concept. One day in a staff meeting at one of the reputedly most advanced hospitals in Scotland, one of the authors was amazed to hear a staff nurse talking about a seventeen-year-old female patient as if 'she was a daughter to me'. The nurse was explaining why he did not want her to leave the hospital, even though she was fit to do so. He was attempting to protect her against the 'cruel hard world' outside. 'And anyway,' he added, 'if she does leave, she will only be replaced by another mental patient.'

Bearing in mind this principle, it may become a little easier to understand one of the great mysteries of the field of mental health. The hospitals' claims to existence rest on the fallacy that they treat their patients, and that their patients get better. The reality is that little treatment is carried out, and many patients get worse. The conclusions of a carefully controlled experiment with regard to differing treatment modes is clear and emphatic (Pasamanick *et al.*, 1969, pp. 516–23):

> In the hospital, between acute episodes, patients are mostly left alone to stare vacantly into space, to walk down the corridors and back again, to sit, rock, and hallucinate, or to partake of inmate culture. In time, this lack of normal

stimulation – intellectual, inter-personal, even physical – has usually resulted in deterioration and impairment of functioning which was wholly unnecessary. . . . Whatever else may eventuate from this investigation and related studies, one conclusion seems warranted: in the absence of considerable deterioration, an acute episode or grossly exaggerated symptoms, no special reason exists for keeping schizophrenic patients hospitalized. Community facilities now being established and those already in existence, are reasonable, preferable, and necessary.

There is ample literature to provide evidence that the internal structure of the hospital allows the conspiracy to continue even after admittance. Hannah Green's vivid account of life in a mental hospital (1972) gives us a rare insight into the strategies that the patients use to outwit the medical staff. In a sense the patient is once more caught in a bind. In order to enter the hospital in the first place, he had to be defined as sick. In order to leave, he must be re-defined as cured. The progress of the patient's career whilst he is inside the institution is governed by his behaviour. Goffman (1970) speaks of 'personal lines of adaptation' and Scheff (1970) looks at the 'sick role' and how it is maintained through expectations. Thus to a large extent the patient is in control of his own progress. For, unlike the family, the hospital provides strategies for changing behaviour – indeed the only way the patient can leave the hospital is by adapting to one of these strategies.

Meanwhile the family might very well be preparing for the return of the patient from the hospital. This can be a very difficult period, both for the family and the patient. Both family and patient are anxious about each other. If we were to look at an imaginary family and patient, this is what might happen. First the impending arrival of the patient. The family is talking:

MOTHER   Our John comes back today.

FATHER   It's about time.

DAUGHTER (18-years-old)   I have to move my things out of his room.

MOTHER   Yes, you will dear, and make sure you leave it just as he left it.

DAUGHTER   Yes, he always was fussy, wasn't he?

MOTHER   Don't talk like that. I want you and him to be
friends. Especially now. We all have to be extra nice to him.

FATHER   That's right, so watch what you say, girl.

DAUGHTER   So everything is going to be different now, is it?

MOTHER   Of course it is. The doctors say that he is cured. So
be careful how you talk to him when he gets back.

FATHER   We have to forget about the past. It's a new start.
Just make sure you do not mention that girl friend.

MOTHER   That tart. Well, I hope he has better taste now.
And hopefully he will give up those friends. They upset
him so much.

FATHER   Whatever you do, don't mention the hospital. It's
best forgotten, and we don't want to upset him, do we?

The patient will be just as concerned about returning home as
the family is:

JOHN (20-years-old)   I bet it will still be the same. Mother
still won't let me do anything. And Father will agree just
the same as always. Always agrees just for the sake of
peace. But it will be good to see Sis again, though I wish
she would not agree with Mum and Dad so much. It'll be
good to see the old crowd again. I've missed my friends
whilst I've been in here. And it will be good to have my
own room once again. I really should be nicer to Mum and
Dad, after all, they are getting on.

In this third part, the patient has returned home and the whole
family are waiting for him to come downstairs:

JOHN   What's happened to my room? It's different!

MOTHER   Why, nothing dear, it's the same as always.

JOHN   Everything has been moved. I can't find anything.

SISTER   You just think that. Nobody has been in there.

JOHN   OK. OK. OK. OK.

FATHER   Now, we've got to start thinking about the future.
What are you going to do, son?

MOTHER   He just got home, don't rush him. There is plenty
of time for that tomorrow.

FATHER   I just want what's best for him. I'm only trying to help.

JOHN   I thought a lot about that while I was in hospital –

MOTHER (*not listening*)   Would you like some tea dear?

JOHN   You're not listening to me Mother.

MOTHER   I know dear, but first things first. Do you still take two sugars?

JOHN   (*shouting*)   You never did listen to me! It's the same as always!

SISTER   Here we go again.

FATHER   Shut up girl. Look son, don't talk to your Mother like that. I won't stand for it.

JOHN   I'm going out.

FATHER   I suppose you are going to see those friends of yours, aren't you. And that girl.

MOTHER   Why can't we all sit down for dinner? I want it to be nice. I have a special roast and some of your favourite sweet. (*John grabs his coat and runs out.*)

The above conversation is not far-fetched. It will happen time and again, with many variations. For the real difficulty is that the problems within the family have not been examined and brought to light. The 'mental patient' returns to a virtually unchanged milieu. At best, this process is a kind of patchwork. If the theory is correct, a dramatic change is required in the approach to the whole field of mental health: and here are some of the changes that would have to be made to implement this. First of all, no individual would be given treatment on his own unless he was living on his own. No individual would be labelled, and removed from his home to a hospital (the exception being where the individual stated that he wanted a place of sanctuary for himself). Obviously most hospitals would have to close down, and those remaining change their functions drastically. No individual would be forced to receive treatment unless his behaviour hurt other people. All treatment would take place in the home or in small social centres, the essential difference being that the individual would not be isolated from his community but rather that his family, friends, neighbours and workmates would be encouraged to share in helping this person. Problems would not be seen and treated in isolation. This would obviously involve changes in the law, in administration, the role of the police and of everyone involved in the keeping professions.

Unless the change does happen, the whole fabric of society is liable to collapse.

Alternatives for growth

It is difficult to be a good listener. And good listening is the basis for all good communication. There are two basic ways by which we hear what another person is saying. One is the intellectual level, the other is the emotional level. Either of these levels can be disturbed fairly easily. If, for example, we move into a situation where we feel we have to prove ourselves, it is easy to begin competing rather than listening. In this way we are more interested in scoring points over the other person than in listening to what they are trying to say.

On the feeling level, the disruption can be more subtle and yet more violent. This is because it is not always obvious; it may be very well hidden – even from ourselves. One example of this kind of problem in communication is where the feelings which have not been dealt with from a situation which has happened before have spilled over onto a present event. For example, at breakfast a husband might shout and grow very angry with his wife because she has burned the toast. The real issue, however, may be that he had wanted to make love to her that morning but she had refused. This made him feel very frustrated, but it was a feeling he could not cope with at the time, so he deals with it in this way instead.

Listening is very difficult for all the members of the Tyrone family. Mary's complete and absolute denial of Edmund's illness is the classic example in the play. Even when Edmund tells her directly that he has got to go to a sanatorium, she refuses to listen:

EDMUND (*then with a bitter stubbornness persists*) Listen Momma. I'm going to tell you whether you want to hear or not. I've got to go to a sanatorium.

MARY (*dazedly, as if this was something that had never occurred to her*) Go away? (*Violently.*) No! I won't have it! How dare doctor Hardy advise such a thing without consulting me! How dare your Father allow him! What right has he? You are my baby! Let him attend to Jamie! (*More and more excited and bitter.*) I know why he wants you sent to a sanatorium. To take you from me! He's always tried to do that. He's been jealous of every one of my babies! He kept finding ways to make me leave them. That's what caused Eugene's death. He's been jealous of you most of all. He knew I loved you most because –

EDMUND (*miserably*) Oh, stop talking crazy, can't you Momma! Stop trying to blame him. And why are you so against my going away now? I've been away a lot, and never noticed it to break your heart!

MARY (*bitterly*) I'm afraid you're not very sensitive after all. (*Sadly.*) You might have guessed dear that after I knew that you knew – about me – I had to be glad wherever you were where you couldn't see me.

EDMUND (*brokenly*) Momma! Don't! (*He reaches out blindly and takes her hand – but he drops it immediately, overcome by bitterness again.*) All this talk about loving me – and you won't even listen when I try to tell you how sick –

MARY (*with an abrupt transformation into a detached, bullying motherliness*) Now, now. That's enough! I don't care to hear because I know it is nothing but Hardy's ignorant lies.

(*He shrinks back into himself. She keeps on in a forced, teasing tone but with an increased undercurrent of resentment.*)

You're so like your father dear. You love to make a scene out of nothing so you can be dramatic and tragic. (*With a belittling laugh.*) If I gave you the slightest encouragement, you would tell me next that you were going to die –

EDMUND People do die of it. Your own father –

MARY (*sharply*) Why do you mention him? There is no comparison at all with you. He had consumption. (*Angrily.*) I hate you when you become gloomy and morbid! I forbid you to remind me of my father's death, do you hear me!

EDMUND (*his face hard – grimly*) Yes, I hear you Momma. I wish to God I didn't! (*He gets up from his chair and stands staring condemningly at her – bitterly.*) It's pretty hard to take at times, having a dope fiend for a Mother!

(pp. 103–5)

Mary's first response is to become very angry. She attempts to blame first of all the doctor, and secondly the father. She is terrified by the thought that Edmund might die – which in those days (1912) was a distinct possibility. Her fear is further strengthened by the fact that her father died of the same disease. Mary over-reacts. Edmund makes a simple statement of truth – painful no doubt, but a truth that has been known for some time. But the mother's response is to simply explode into anger. The news is so painful for her emotionally, that she attempts to rationalize it away intellectually by denial. She hits out at everything – first of all the doctor, then the father.

Shortly after lunch Mary says that she is going up to her room. The others are all suspicious of the reason:

MARY   I'm going upstairs for a moment, if you'll excuse me. I have to fix my hair. (*She adds smilingly.*) That is if I can find my glasses. I'll be right down.

TYRONE (*as she starts through the doorway – pleading and rebuking*)   Mary!

MARY (*turns to stare at him calmly*)   Yes, dear? What is it?

TYRONE (*helplessly*)   Nothing.

MARY (*with a strange derisive smile*)   You are welcome to come up and watch me if you are so suspicious.

TYRONE   As if that would do any good! You'd only postpone it. And I'm not your jailer. This isn't a prison.

MARY   No. I know you can't help thinking it's a home. (*She adds quickly with a detached contrition.*) I'm sorry dear. I don't mean to be bitter. It's not your fault.

(*She turns and disappears through the back parlor. The three in the room remain silent. It is as if they were waiting until she got upstairs before speaking.*)

JAMIE (*cynically brutal*)   Another shot in the arm!

EDMUND (*angrily*)   Cut out that kind of talk!

TYRONE   Yes! Hold your foul tongue and your rotten Broadway-loafers lingo! Have you no pity or decency? (*Losing his temper.*) You ought to be kicked out into the gutter! But if I did it, you know damn well who'd weep and plead for you, and excuse you and complain until I let you come back.

JAMIE (*a spasm of pain crosses his face*)   Christ, don't I know that? No pity? I have all the pity in the world for her. I understand what a hard game to beat she is up against – which is more than you ever have!

(pp. 64–5)

Everyone knows that Mary is high on drugs at this point, and that in all probability she is going upstairs to her room to fix once more. But no one is prepared to be open and confronting. When

Jamie makes the most honest statement, albeit cynically, he is told to shut up.

For the moment, let us look at some of the alternatives the Tyrones might have followed in both these examples and the consequences that might have followed. We would like to concentrate on how the closed system of the Tyrones might become open, thus allowing for the growth of the individual.

Edmund must come to terms with death, just as everyone must. Thus it is imperative that he share the doctor's news with his mother. In this way it could be possible for the emotional bond between mother and son to be strengthened. For Edmund could receive sympathy and understanding to ease his own suffering and he in turn could be able to offer strength and affection to his mother. Thus, when faced with a denial, perhaps the ideal course for Edmund to have followed would have been to have shown a great tolerance and sympathy for his mother's pain.

In the second example we are faced with the whole family colluding with the mother's self-destruction. They claim to love, but do nothing. How could they have handled it differently? We suggest by being generally more open and honest with their feelings. When Mary goes to leave the room, they all know what she is going for but only the father alludes to the possible reason and he quickly backs off. The two sons remain silent. Surely the family would want to get Mary to share with them what she was feeling and also attempt to make the whole issue open so that it could be discussed. Inherent in behaving in this way would be the message that they wanted Mary's love and affection for themselves, which would value her. To begin on this course would mean that all the taboo areas would have to be removed and genuine growth could begin. Only in this way is the separateness and uniqueness of the individual recognized, and his independence retained.

It is not the actual conflicts themselves which made the Tyrone family disturbed, but rather the way in which they handled them. Almost every family will have its conflicts from time to time. This is because a family is never static. And for this reason the idea of negotiation is of great importance. Thus the conflict will be shared, the alternative renewed and a new contract made. In this way growth and change are recognized as dynamic factors, and negotiation is the means whereby the integrity of the individual family member is maintained.

4 THE LOMAN FAMILY

Death of a Salesman by Arthur Miller

List of characters

Willy Loman   Bernard
Linda   The Woman
Biff   Letta
Happy

Synopsis of the plot of the play

This is the story of Willy Loman, an American salesman and his family. It is the story of a man's fight for survival in the big city 'jungle'. Willy, in his role as a salesman, tries to imbue his two sons with a recipe for success when, in effect, he is anything but a success himself. In fact, as the play unfolds, we see that the family realizes that Willy is a failure and do their best to try and shield him from the verities of a cruel world. At different times, Willy uses fantasy to try to convince himself and his family that all is well, that Willy is the best salesman in the world. But in the end, even Willy must deal with reality and one final act of self-destruction works it out so that his son can carry on after him, to prove to himself that his son had finally made the big time.

Portrait of a salesman

When *Death of a Salesman* had been playing for only a few weeks in New York, it made such a profound impact on the sales-field that more than a few salesmen quit their jobs. Writing in the *New York Times*, 11 February 1949, the well known drama critic Brooks Atkinson, had this to say about the play: 'Mr Miller has looked with compassion into the hearts of ordinary Americans and quietly transferred their hope and anguish to the theatre.'

The American salesman has always been a somewhat suspicious character. A successful salesman is represented as a 'smoothy'. He is well dressed, charming, intelligent and has a good personality. He is friendly to dogs and children. Some housewives find him extremely attractive. Psychiatrists have often equated salesmanship with psychopathy. There is an old adage – never talk to a salesman, he will try to sell you something. His purpose is to establish a particular kind of business contact – your money is his business.

Thus, the status of a salesman is suspect or, at least, a marginal one. We only have to think of the used car salesman or the man who sells ladies' underwear. Both are victims of a different kind of suspicion. If we meet the used car salesman, we might put our hands on our wallets in an attempt to hold on to what we have or, in the other case, we might look askance and think if our wives and daughters are safe.

Why do men become salesmen? Despite the above dismal picture, there appears to be no shortage of applicants. The job offers travel, good money, a chance to meet unusual people and the opportunity to be independent and responsible for oneself.

The dilemma that the salesman faces is how to integrate these two aspects – the attraction of the job coupled with the suspicions it raises in the minds of the people. Willy Loman represents one such attempt:

> I realized that selling was the greatest career a man could want. 'Cause what could be more satisfying than to be able to go at the age of eighty-four, into twenty or thirty different cities, and pick up a phone, and be remembered and loved and helped by so many different people?' Do you know? when he died – and by the way, he died the death of a salesman, in his green velvet slippers in the smoker of the New York, New Haven and Hartford, going into Boston – when he died, hundreds of salesmen and buyers were at his funeral. Things were said on a lotta trains for months after that. (*He stands up. Howard has not looked at him.*) In those days, there was personality in it, Howard. There was respect, and comradeship, and gratitude in it.

(p. 63)

Willy Loman represents such an attempt. He has a dream; to him the life of a salesman possesses almost the quality of the myth. The dream is to be a salesman who is loved – the salesman who achieves wealth, status and the respect of his trade and all his customers. One might say that his ambition is to be everybody's friend. This is one of Willy's fantasies that fails. The dream becomes a tragedy, when the salesman, in a last desperate attempt to maintain the dream for his family, commits suicide by crashing his car against a wall.

Freud states that everyone needs work and love to survive. It is impossible to separate completely the life of the man at work and the man with his family. In *Death of a Salesman* these two themes are deeply involved with each other and affect each other. With the Loman family, we will analyse the importance of fantasy, the deadly consequences of secrets, how difficult it is for one family member to allow for differences in another family member. We shall also draw heavily from Ibsen's *The Wild Duck* to emphasize the concepts of secrets and self-esteem. The other things we shall be writing about are what expectations mean in the Loman family and the role of the model child. We begin with a discussion of the concept of the 'work role', and its implications for family life.

Work role

Retirement leads to death. Table 1 demonstrates the steep rise in the death rate, particularly for men, in the 65–9 age group. Significantly, this is also the age group in which the vast majority of men retire.

Max Weber, the German sociologist, was one of the first thinkers to point out the massive importance of the work ethic. In his work *Protestant Ethic and the Spirit of Capitalism* (1970 edn), he stresses the importance of work in our society and indicates how this was achieved in relation to Protestantism.

Since Weber's time, the nature of work has undergone dramatic change. Where once a seven-day 80-hour week and degrading working conditions prevailed, we now have the four-day week. In some instances, the influence of work, through organized trade unions, coupled with huge technological changes, has almost reversed its former position. One might almost say that today

131

leisure time rather than work is the great problem.

Still today, men feel that it is vital for them to work. The effects of mass unemployment lead to demoralization. Men are prepared to go to prison in order to maintain their jobs. This was demonstrated during the dock strike in England in 1972. Here, six men

Table 1   Death rate related to age and sex

Age	Sex	Total deaths	Total deaths expressed as rate per 1,000
60–4	M	36,328	27·8
60–4	F	19,534	13·1
65–9	M	46,698	45·6
65–9	F	28,625	22·0
70–4	M	45,227	70·4
70–4	F	38,594	36·7

Figures: *Registrar General's Statistical Review for England and Wales*, 1969, Part I; Tables – medical, published 1971, Table 17 – Death by cause, sex and age group, 1969, p. 117.

were imprisoned because they insisted on refusing to allow an outside agency to do certain work. Their behaviour was in direct contradiction to a ruling made by the Industrial Relations Board. Hence, they were imprisoned. The reason they behaved as they did was tied in with the decline of dock work over the past years. They believed that by allowing an outside company to become involved with dock-side work, they would lose their jobs. Work is part of man's self-respect. By and large, he is still the provider and, with some exceptions, it is important for him to maintain this role. Few men would be happy if they felt they had to be supported by the State – probably even less so by their wives. Anthony Jay in his book *Corporation Man* (1972), claims that the corporation employee is still living a life style similar to that of his primitive ancestors. He is a hunter, his salary is his prize, and the material things that money can buy are the symbols of his hunting ability. The analogy may be amusing, but in the light of the way many workers behave, at times it might not seem so far-fetched. The man who does not work is a figure of suspicion and even contempt by his peers. Work is an integral part of our identity. It gives us status, self-respect, self-esteem and respect from others. Part of

Willy Loman's problem is the difference between what he does and what he would like to do. As the play opens, Willy appears completely exhausted. His wife is concerned:

LINDA Don't you feel well?

WILLY I'm tired to the death. (*The flute has faded away. He sits on the bed beside her, a little numb.*) I couldn't make it. I just couldn't make it, Linda.

LINDA But you're sixty years old. They can't expect you to keep travelling every week.

(pp. 8, 10)

What has happened to the Willy who said:

> . . . Tell you a secret, boys. Don't breathe it to a soul. Someday I'll have my own business, and I'll never have to leave home anymore.

(p. 23)

Willy's dream of his job may have crumbled and he may be down, but like a good fighter he remains undefeated. He still feels that it is possible to get the ideal job, the position of importance which will help him fulfil his desire for stature and influence. He talks to his wife about applying for a new job:

WILLY Gee Whiz! That's really somethin: I'm gonna knock Howard for a loop, kid. I'll get an advance and I'll come home with a New York job. Goddam it! Now I'm gonna do it!

LINDA Oh that's the spirit, Willy!

WILLY I will never get behind a wheel the rest of my life!

LINDA It's changing, Willy, I can feel it changing!

WILLY Beyond a question. G'bye. I'm late. (*He starts to go again.*)

(pp. 57–8)

It is important for a man to have dreams. When Willy first started, he had dreams. . . . Ben has just offered Willy a job in Alaska to look after his business interests:

LINDA (*frightened of Ben and angry at him*) Don't say those things to him! Enough to be happy right here, right now. (*To Willy, while Ben laughs.*) Why must everybody conquer the world? You're well liked and the boys love you and someday (*to Ben*) why old man Wagner told him just the other day, that if he keeps it up he'll be a member of the firm, didn't he Willy?

WILLY   Sure, sure. I am building something with this firm, Ben, and if a man is building something he must be on the right track, mustn't he?

(p. 67)

But what has happened to Willy's dreams? We see a very different Willy in a special interview with his boss when Willy says:

WILLY   Remember, Christmas-time, when you had the party here? You said you'd try to think of some spot for me here in town.

HOWARD   With us?

WILLY   Well, sure.

HOWARD   Oh, yeah, yeah. I remember. Well, I couldn't think of anything for you, Willy.

WILLY   I tell ya, Howard. The kids are all grown up, y'know. I don't need much any more. If I could take home – well 65.00 a week, I could swing it.

WILLY   God knows, Howard, I never asked a favour of any man. But I was with the firm when your father used to carry you in here in his arms. . . . (*With increasing anger.*) Howard, all I need to set my table is fifty dollars a week.

HOWARD   But where am I going to put you, kid?

WILLY   Look, it isn't a question of whether I can sell merchandise, is it?

HOWARD   No, but it's a business, kid, and everybody's gotta pull his own weight.

(p. 62)

Willy now becomes a beggar:

WILLY   If I had forty dollars a week – that's all I'd need, forty dollars, Howard.

HOWARD   Kid, I can't take blood from a stone, I –

(p. 64)

Howard won't meet Willy's request. In face of Howard's adamant refusal, Willy resigns himself to going back to his old job. But his shame is not complete. He is further humiliated:

WILLY   I'll go to Boston.

HOWARD   Willy, you can't go to Boston for us.

WILLY   Why can't I go?

HOWARD   I don't want you to represent us. I've been meaning to tell you for a long time now.

WILLY   Howard, are you firing me?

HOWARD   I think you need a good long rest, Willy.

WILLY   Howard. . . .

HOWARD   And when you feel better, come back, and we'll see if we can work something out.

WILLY   But I gotta earn money, Howard. I'm in no position. . . .

HOWARD   Where are your sons? Why don't your sons give you a hand?

WILLY   I can't throw myself on my sons. I'm not a cripple!

HOWARD   Look, kid, I'm busy this morning.

WILLY (*grasping Howard's arm*)   Howard, you got to let me go to Boston!

HOWARD (*hard – keeping himself under control*)   I've got a line of people to see this morning. Sit down. Take five minutes and pull yourself together, then go home, will ya! I need the office, Willy.

(pp. 65–6)

When this happens to a man he must not only face himself but also his family. When a man is like Willy and a job is the central part of his life, this must be doubly horrifying because his degradation is so much more complete. And under the circumstances, the whole family becomes the victim. Willy goes from the interview to meet his sons:

BIFF (*high, slightly alcoholic, above the earth*)   I'm going to tell you everything from first to last. It's been a strange day. (*Silence. He looks round, composes himself as best he can, but his breath keeps breaking the rhythm of his voice.*) I had to wait quite a while for him, and –

WILLY   Oliver?

BIFF Yeah. Oliver. All day as a matter of cold fact. And a lot of – instances – facts, Pop, facts about my life came back to me. Who was it, Pop? Who said I was a salesman with Oliver?

WILLY Well, you were.

BIFF No, Dad, I was a shipping clerk.

WILLY But you were practically. . . .

BIFF (*with determination*) Dad, I don't know who said it first, but I was never a salesman for Bill Oliver.

WILLY What're you talking about?

BIFF Let's hold onto the facts tonight, Pop. We're not going to get anywhere bullin' around. I was a shipping clerk.

WILLY (*angrily*) All right! Now listen to me.

BIFF Why don't you let me finish?

WILLY I'm not interested in stories about the past or any crap of that kind because the woods are burning, boys, you understand? There's a big blaze going on all around. I was fired today.

BIFF (*shocked*) How could you be?

WILLY I was fired and I'm looking for a little good news to tell your Mother, because the woman has waited and the woman has suffered. The gist of it is that I haven't got a story left in my head, Biff. So don't give me a lecture about facts and aspects. I am not interested. Now what've you got to say to me?

(p. 84)

Willy has never faced reality. He has built a life on dreams. Now his job is gone and he can only live on charity. His humiliation is complete.

In this next section we move away from external influences, and use the concept of 'expectations' to examine some of the internal dynamics of family life. This concept is particularly important in the field of education.

Expectations

When we meet a person who has an obvious and visible label, such as a nun or a priest, we tend to modify our own behaviour, such as speech patterns, in accordance with what we think is expected. At the same time we make demands on them. We strongly expect them to meet our image. In this way a role is maintained and often a stereotype will develop. The same thing occurs but in more subtle ways with others who have labels such as a doctor, mental patient, criminal, policeman (the latter whether he is in or out of uniform). A good example of this occurred when an anthropologist decided to study a psychiatric ward in a mental hospital. William Caudill decided the best way to conduct his study would be to be admitted as a patient. The remarkable thing was that after a short time there, he was labelled 'psychopathic'. This is like saying that from the point of view of the medical staff, anyone who lives in the ward must automatically be sick. The eminent American sociologist Thomas Scheff has incorporated these ideas into a theoretical model. He says (1970): 'These considerations suggest that the labelling process is a crucial contingency in most careers of residual deviants. . . . That is, their deviance is stabilized by the labelling process, which is implicit in their removal and hospitalization.'

If Scheff's hypothesis is at all accurate (and there is increasing evidence to support this), this has great implications for the study of communication in the family. It means we must pay close attention to the expectations the members place on each other.

Before we begin a study of the Loman family, it will be valuable to examine this concept which we feel is vital to the child's development, and in another area that is crucial to the child's development, the school. In the discussion of self-esteem, we have already mentioned the nature of the self-fulfilling prophecy relative to the British education system. Those children that failed the exam were told at the outset that they were expected to do far less well than those who passed. There are a great many recent studies which all show the same thing regarding expectations. Probably the most famous of these is *Pygmalion in the Classroom* by Robert Rosenthal and Lenore Jacobsen, in which a number of children in a selected group had their IQ scores raised by as much as 69 points because a high set of expectations were placed on them.

But if we expect the child to fail or do poorly, he most certainly will. A startling individual example is related by Herbert Kohl in his book *Thirty-six Children* (1972). He tells us of a twelve-year-old girl who is described as having a reading ability compared to someone in the third grade. One day during the first week, Alice proposed a bet (Kohl, 1972, p. 189):

> 'Mr Kohl, I bet I can read anything on your desk no matter what those cards of yours say.' Her reading score was 3·4.
> I accepted and she went through all the books on my desk including the page of the novel I was reading on the way to school. I was perplexed and delighted. 'How can you do that and still have a 3·4 reading score?' 'I wouldn't read to those teachers. Listen.' Alice picked up a book and stumbled through several paragraphs. She paused, stuttered, committed reversals and omissions, i.e., read on a low third grade level. Then she looked at my astonished face and burst out laughing. Alice was tough and angry and brilliant. She was hypersensitive and incapable of tolerating insult or prejudice. In her previous year in school she had been alternately defiant and withdrawn. She was considered a 'trouble-maker' by some teachers, 'disturbed' by others. When offered something substantial, a serious novel, for example, or the opportunity to write honestly, she blossomed. During the year she became hungry to learn and less hostile. It was sometimes hard to find material to keep up with her voracious appetite.

Alice acted dumb because this was what the teachers expected of her. Though she was never told directly, none the less she obviously received very clear messages in some way that she was expected to be a very poor reader. If we explore Kohl a little further, we get some inkling of the process by which this took place (1972, p. 88):

> The following September meant meeting new children, concentrating my energy and feeling on them and letting go of my pre-occupation on the thirty-six children. It was sad yet exciting, beginning again with an empty classroom. I waited nervously for the children, refusing to think of my first words. At nine o'clock they came in quietly and hesitantly, looking me over. They were nervous too. I felt free to encounter the children without preconceptions.

Other teachers had warned me of my new class – it was 'the bottom'. I was told the children were illiterate, indifferent, dangerous. Someone claimed that most of them wouldn't even show-up after the first week. In June some colleagues, as the children expected, offered to point out 'the ones' who would cause me the most trouble. I declined just as I had declined to look at the children's records in September. The children looked older than the ones in six-minus-one, taller and more self-assured. They spoke about themselves freely and with great perception. They knew they were rejects in the school and they also knew that the school, as a whole, was a reject. Any adult pretence of the opposite would have closed them up altogether. As soon as everyone was settled, I began as directly as possible and asked the class what books they wanted to read. Naturally, they asked for sixth grade readers. I told them that I felt the books were too hard and they groaned. 'We are not so dumb, Mr Kohl.' 'I won't chew that baby stuff again.' 'Mr Kohl, we can read anything.' I asked the children how well they thought they read and they became confused, no one had ever told them. They only knew that every year they got the same second and third grade books, which they knew by heart. My first lesson became clear. I took out the class record cards and put them on my desk. Then I explained to the class what grade reading scores meant, and what the significance of IQ was. 'If you are reading up to your grade level, that means the sixth grade, you are supposed to have a score in the sixes: 6·0, 6·1, and so forth. If you have average intelligence your IQ should be at least 100. Let's see what these cards say.'

There was suspense in the room as I listed the scores: '3·1, 3·4, 2·0, 4·2, 3·1. . . . IQ's of 70, 75, 81, 78. . . .' Then anger. 'Mr Kohl, we're not that dumb.' 'It's phoney.' 'No one taught us that stuff, no one ever told us.' But they knew now. After a heated debate, I threw my first question back at the class 'Tell me what books you want to read?' The class chose fifth grade readers, ones they knew would be difficult for them in preference to ones that were on their supposed 'level'. They were ready to fight, to read and learn, met my challenge, kept on challenging themselves and me for the rest of the year.

The pupils may be confused, but the teachers are very clear. In the privacy of the staff room, the new teacher is quickly indoctrinated. He is immediately informed who are the good pupils, the bad pupils, the trouble-makers. In this way a myth is created and maintained. The pupil is trapped in a low expectation. The only way he can escape is by some new influence. The same kind of process can go on in the family. Often, low expectations are communicated by a series of confused messages. The process can be exceedingly subtle. For example, in working with this type of family a number of years ago, one of the authors had the following experience.

The family included a mother and father and young boy of sixteen. The boy had been referred to us by Court Order for stealing cars and running away from school. The programme was a residential one and the families met once-weekly with the boys. During one of the sessions, the question of schooling was discussed. The boy had been asked how he felt about attending school and he replied 'So so'. In asking his mother how she let her son know that school was important, she said 'Oh, I tell him every day it's very important'. I pursued the question a little further and asked about the interaction at home when the boy came home from school. The boy replied at some point that he would come home from school, drop his books off in the dining room, ask for some food and tell his mother that he would be going out to play, that he would do his home-work later. The mother would then accept this response and say something to the effect that 'Well, your Uncle Harry didn't go to school, and it didn't seem to have done him any harm. In fact, he seems to be quite successful today.' (Uncle Harry was an automobile salesman.) Given this message, and the fact that the Uncle was a significant person for the young boy, it is no wonder that the boy received confused communication from his mother concerning the value of school.

These two forces, the school and the home, are the major influences in developing the child's image of himself. Thus, for example, if the school and the home working in concert, covertly tell the child that he is extremely limited, then the child has little choice but to internalize these expectations – he is a victim. In the

Loman family we are presented with what appears to be a paradox. On the one hand the parents appear to have almost fanatically high expectations for their son Biff. And yet at 33 he is a thief and a wandering farm hand. How could this come about?

Willy's ambitions appear to be very clear. He continually tells his son that he is going to be a great success. Willy is talking to his two sons and their school friend, Bernard, shortly before a football game:

BIFF   Oh, Pop, you didn't see my sneakers!
(*He holds up a foot for Willy to look at.*)
WILLY   Hey, that's a beautiful job of printing!
BERNARD (*wiping his glasses*) Just because he printed University of Virginia on his sneakers, doesn't mean they've got to graduate him, Uncle Willy!
WILLY (*angrily*)   What're you talking about? With scholarships to three Universities they're gonna flunk him?
BERNARD   But I heard Mr Birnbaum say –
WILLY   Don't be a pest, Bernard! (*To his boys.*) What an anaemic!
BERNARD   Okay, I'm waiting for you in my house, Biff.
(*Bernard goes off. The Lomans laugh.*)
WILLY   Bernard is not well-liked, is he?
HAPPY   That's right, Pop.
WILLY   That's just what I mean. Bernard can get the best marks in school, y'understand, but when he gets out in the business world, y'understand, you are going to be five times ahead of him. That's why I thank Almighty God you're both built like Adonises. Because the man who makes an appearance in the business world, the man who creates personal interest, is the man who gets ahead. Be liked and you will never want. You take me, for instance. I never have to wait in line to see a buyer. 'Willy Loman is here!' That's all they have to know, and I go right through.

(p. 25)

Willy is confident and cannot fathom failure with Biff. But is he being realistic? What message is Willy really giving Biff? He completely rejects attempts to bring him down to earth:

> BERNARD Biff! (*He gets away from Happy.*) Listen, Biff, I
> heard Mr Birnbaum say if you don't start studyin' math,
> he's gonna flunk you, and you won't graduate. I heard
> him!
> WILLY You better study with him, Biff. Go ahead now.
>
> (p. 25)

On the surface this would seem to be a clear expectation on
Willy's part that he expects Biff to work hard. But we have already
seen in the previous quote that Willy disqualifies Bernard. Later,
Willy's real attitudes become much more clear when he sees the
danger that Biff might fail his exam. His response is to advocate
cheating by directly ordering Bernard to give him the answers
during the mathematics examination.

Biff is the loved one. What Willy is saying is that because Biff
is attractive, charming and good at football, he is bound to be a
success. There is no need to work. Reward will follow. This is
almost completely unrealistic. Later on, it is Bernard who succeeds
while Biff is a failure. The same confused communication can
take place in the area of morality. This is completely clear in the
Loman family in connection with stealing. In an attempt to
impress Ben, Willy sends his boys off to steal some sand from a
building site:

> WILLY Boys! Go right over to where they're building the
> apartment house and get some sand. We're gonna rebuild
> the entire front stoop right now! Watch this, Ben!
> BIFF Yes sir! On the double, Hap!
> HAPPY (*as he and Biff run off*) I lost weight, Pop you notice?
> (*Charley enters in knickers, even before the boys are gone.*)
> CHARLEY Listen, if they steal any more from that building,
> the watchman'll put the cops on them!
> LINDA (*to Willy*) Don't let Biff. . . .
> (*Ben laughs lustily.*)
> WILLY You should a seen the lumber they brought home
> last week. At least a dozen six-by-tens worth all kinds a
> money.
> CHARLEY Listen, if that watchman. . . .
> WILLY I gave them hell, understand. But I got a couple of
> fearless characters there.
>
> (p. 39)

When this kind of communication goes on long enough the message is that stealing is OK.

In another illustrative case history, in discussing the delinquency of a 17-year-old boy, the mother related that the child had a history of stealing. She stated that when her son was 7 years old, he would come home with packages of candy and she would ask him where he got the candy. He would smile and say that a man had given the candy to him. This happened so frequently that it was pretty obvious that the boy had been stealing the candy rather than it being given to him by an assortment of men. Each time the boy returned home with candy, the mother would smile and say to the boy 'I know really where you got that candy, naughty, naughty boy, you should not do that'. At the same time that she was admonishing him for stealing candy, she was smiling with obvious approval. In the session, the boy related how he had been taking drugs, stealing cars and been involved in other kinds of delinquency. While discussing these events, the mother smiled during almost the entire session. When asked what kind of message she was giving her son as he was relating the delinquent events, she would simply smile and say 'I love him, he's my son'. It was interesting that this woman rationalized the stealing of cars by her son by stating that 'Everyone has insurance, isn't that right'.

In the face of this kind of communication, it is little wonder that the child becomes delinquent. In the Loman family, Willy pleads innocence and cannot at all see his part in teaching his son a confused value system. He disclaims, 'Why is he stealing? What did I tell him, I never in my life told him other than decent things.' The whole confusion is eloquently captured when Willy is told about all the things that Biff is doing wrong by his wife and Bernard:

BERNARD (*entering on the run*) Where is he? If he doesn't study!

WILLY (*moving to the fore-stage with great agitation*) You'll give him the answers!

BERNARD I do but I can't on a Regents! That's a state exam! They're liable to arrest me!

WILLIE   Where is he? I'll whip him, I'll whip him!

LINDA   And he'd better give back that football, Willy, it's not nice.

WILLY   Biff! Where is he? Why is he taking everything?

LINDA   He's too rough with the girls, Willy. All the mothers are afraid of him.

BERNARD   He's driving the car without a licence!

(*The woman's laugh is heard.*)

WILLY   Shut up!

LINDA   All the mothers –

WILLY   Shut up!

BERNARD (*backing quietly away and out*)   Mr Birnbaum says he's stuck-up.

WILLY   Get outa here!

BERNARD   If he doesn't buckle down he'll flunk math!

(*He goes off.*)

LINDA   He's right, Willy, you've gotta.

WILLY (*exploding at her*)   There's nothing the matter with him! You want him to be a worm like Bernard? He's got spirit, personality. . . . (*As he speaks, Linda almost in tears, exits to the living room. Willy is alone in the kitchen, writing and staring. The leaves are gone. It is night again, and the apartment houses look down from behind.*)

(p. 31)

With such massive confusion and contradictory expectations, it is a miracle that Biff survives at all. We have shown how confused expectations can be highly destructive. However, when expectations are clearly and positively communicated, the potential which can be realized might almost seem miraculous. We only have to think of the example of Helen Keller to realize this. Helen Keller was born blind and deaf, and was virtually dumb until the arrival of Anne Sullivan. Mrs Sullivan, with devotion and persistence, continually placed high demands on her charge. The result was that a seven-year-old child, with everything against her, graduated from Radcliffe College with the highest honours, and became a world famous lecturer and writer (see Helen Keller, *The Story of My Life*, 1947).

Expectations have to do with what we want from a person, or what we want them to become. Perhaps of even more basic importance is accepting the fact that everyone is different.

Differentness

In our society, it can be a crime to be different. There are certain actions which people become involved in willingly and freely and yet which may be punishable by law if they are caught. These 'crimes without victims' may include abortion, prostitution, drug taking, and homosexuality, for example. The strangest thing about the legal status of these activities is that it differs from country to country. Perhaps no nation quite captures the paradoxical nature of such legislation as does the USA. If we examine homosexuality, for example, we find the following statement (Morris and Hawkins, 1970):

> Homosexual offences are treated under such titles as Sodomy, Buggery, Perverse or Unnatural Acts, and Crimes Against Nature; homosexual practices are condemned in all States with the exception of Illinois, usually as a felony. Penalties vary enormously. A consentual homosexual act which is legal in Illinois, is a misdeameanour in New York and can be punished as a felony by life imprisonment in some States.

The law is often a reflection of the morals held dear by the majority of people. In the example we have quoted above, where no one is likely to be hurt except maybe the people involved, out of a mixture of fear and concern, society gets itself up as a moral judge and says 'We know what is best for you'. This also happens in families.

In the previously mentioned film *Family Life*, directed by Ken Loach, we see this happening when Janice's mother bulldozes the daughter into having an abortion, when clearly the daughter does not want one.

In this film, the mother explicitly tells her daughter that mother knows best. If this were a general rule in families, it would be impossible for children to maintain any kind of separate identity. This is Biff's problem in the Loman family. Since the breakdown in communication between father and son, Biff consistently refuses to follow the ambitions his father maps out for him. He leaves home a number of times, usually following an argument. Each time he returns, he is met with a barrage of recriminations. He is punished for being different. Willy's dream is

for his son Biff to become a great man. He has carried this dream
with him since Biff was a child:

> WILLY Without a penny to his name, three great Universities
> are begging for him, and from there the sky's the limit,
> because it's not what you do, Ben. It's who you know and
> the smile on your face! It's contacts, Ben, contacts. . . .
> when he walks into a business office his name will sound
> out like a bell and all the doors will be opened to him!
>
> (pp. 67–8)

Willy still carries this dream sixteen years later. But now he is
bitter and disappointed:

> WILLY No, no, some people – some people accomplish
> something. Did Biff say anything after I went this
> morning? . . . (*Worried and angered.*) There's such an
> undercurrent in him. He became a moody man. Did he
> apologize when I left this morning?
> LINDA He was crestfallen, Willy. You know how he admires
> you. I think if he finds himself, then you'll both be happier
> and not fight anymore.
> WILLY How can he find himself on a farm? Is that a life?
> A farmhand? In the beginning, when he was young, I
> thought, well, a young man, it's good for him to tramp
> around, take a lot of different jobs. But it's more than ten
> years now and he has yet to make thirty-five dollars a week.
> LINDA He's finding himself, Willy.
> WILLY Not finding himself at the age of thirty-four is a
> disgrace!
> LINDA Ssh!
> WILLY The trouble is, he's lazy goddammit!
> LINDA Willy, please!
> WILLY Biff is a lazy bum!
>
> (pp. 10–11)

Biff's behaviour is, in fact, an attempt to be different and find
his own way. The only way the parents can come near to accepting
the difference is to intepret this behaviour. They rationalize to
themselves by saying that he is 'lost' or simply a late starter. By
saying this, they are implying that Biff is not in his right senses
and that still they expect him to become the person they want him

to. They completely ignore Biff's wishes. One of the ways of not allowing for differences is to refuse to hear what a person is saying when they are attempting to be different. An example of this occurs in the play. After Biff has been to a former employer, Oliver, in an attempt to borrow money to finance a business venture, Willy and Biff meet for dinner after the interview:

BIFF (*high, slightly alcoholic, above the earth*) I'm going to tell you everything from first to last. It's been a strange day. (*Silence. He looks around and composes himself as best he can but his breath keeps breaking the rhythm of his voice.*) I had to wait quite a while for him and –

WILLY Oliver?

BIFF Yeah, Oliver. All day as a matter of cold fact and a lot of – instances – facts, Pop, facts about my life came back to me. Who was it Pop? Whoever said I was a salesman with Oliver?

WILLY Well you were.

BIFF No, Dad, I was a shipping clerk.

WILLY But you were practically –

BIFF (*with determination*): Dad, I don't know who said it first but I was never a salesman with Bill Oliver.

WILLY What're you talking about?

BIFF Let's hold onto the facts tonight, Pop. We're not going to get anywhere bulling around. I was a shipping clerk.

WILLY (*angrily*) All right. Now listen to me.

BIFF Why don't you let me finish?

WILLY I'm not interested in stories about the past or any crap of that kind because the woods are burning, boys, you understand?

(p. 84)

Why does Willy refuse to listen to what is being said? Why does he insist upon hanging onto his dreams? What is the worst that could happen to the Loman family if Biff was to be allowed to be different? If Biff were allowed to follow his own desires, possibly the worst that could happen is that he would be a lowly farm hand, bumming from job to job. What is so terrible about this? The implications for Willy are much more profound. Biff's refusal to conform to his father's ambitions for him mean two major things to Willy. First, that he has failed as a father, and second, that his

147

own dreams were not realized through his son. He will be forced to face the situation as it really is. Thus by the end of the play, communication between the two has completely broken down. In a last despairing attempt to break out of the fantasy, there is an incredibly painful scene where Biff attempts to confront Willy with his limitations and differentness:

BIFF No, you're going to hear the truth – what you are and what I am!

LINDA Stop it.

WILLY Spite!

HAPPY (*coming down towards Biff*) You cut it now!

BIFF (*to Happy*) The man don't know who we are! The man is gonna know! (*To Willy.*) We never told the truth for ten minutes in this house!

HAPPY We always told the truth!

BIFF (*turning on him*) You big blow, are you the assistant buyer? You're one of the two assistants to the assistant, aren't you!

HAPPY Well, I'm practically –

BIFF You're practically full of it. We all are! And I'm through with it. (*To Willy.*) Now hear this, Willy, this is me.

WILLY I know you.

BIFF You know why I had no address for three months? I stole a suit in Kansas City and I was in jail. (*To Linda, who is sobbing.*) Stop crying. I'm through with it.

(*Linda turns away from them, her hands covering her face.*)

WILLY I suppose that's my fault!

BIFF I stole myself out of every good job since high school.

WILLY And whose fault is that?

BIFF And I never got anywhere because you blew me so full of hot air I could never stand taking orders from anybody! That's whose fault it is!

WILLY I hear that!

LINDA Don't, Biff!

BIFF Its goddam time you heard that! I had to be boss big shot in two weeks and I'm through with it!

WILLY (*with hatred, threateningly*) The door of your life is wide open!

BIFF Pop! I'm a dime a dozen, and so are you!

WILLY (*turning on him now in an uncontrolled outburst*)   I am
not a dime a dozen! I am Willy Loman and you are Biff
Loman!

BIFF   I am not a leader of men, Willy, and neither are you.
You were never anything but a hard-working drummer
who landed in the ash can like all the rest of them! I'm
one dollar an hour, Willy!

WILLY (*directly to Biff*)   You vengeful, spiteful mut!

(*Biff breaks from Happy. Willy, in fright, starts up the stairs. Biff
grabs him.*)

BIFF (*at the peak of his fury*)   Pop, I'm nothing, I'm nothing
Pop. Can't you understand that? There's no spite in it any
more. I'm just what I am, that's all.

(*Biff's fury has spent itself, and he breaks down, sobbing, holding
on to Willy, who dumbly fumbles for Biff's face.*)

WILLY   What're you doing? What're you doing? (*To Linda.*)
Why is he crying?

Willy still doesn't hear. Biff leaves the room and Willy comes
out:

WILLY   Oh, Biff! (*Staring wildly.*) He cried! Cried to me. (*He
is choking with his love, and now cries out his promise.*) That
boy – that boy is going to be magnificent. (*Ben appears in
the light just outside the kitchen.*)

(pp. 104–6)

At all costs, Biff must not be different. To demonstrate this and
to hold onto his dream, Willy commits suicide so that his son can
have the insurance money:

WILLY   Can you imagine that magnificence with twenty
thousand dollars in his pocket?

LINDA (*calling from her room*)   Willy! Come up!

WILLY (*calling into the kitchen*)   Yes! Yes. Coming! It's
very smart, you realize that, don't you sweetheart? Even
Ben sees it. I gotta go baby. Bye! Bye! (*Going over to Ben,
almost dancing.*) Imagine? When the mail comes he'll be
ahead of Bernard again!

BEN   A perfect proposition all around.

WILLY   Did you see how he cried to me? Oh, if I could kiss
him, Ben!

BEN Time, William, time!
WILLY Oh Ben, I always knew one way or another we were
　going to make it, Biff and I!

(p. 107)

Even in death, Willy, in his own mind, denies Biff the right to
be different. The right to be different carries with it a price. In
social terms, because of strong opposition, it may lead to alienation, imprisonment, mental hospital or even death. The price of
maintaining one's integrity in the face of opposition is never low.
There is a famous French case where a school teacher was hounded
to death because she chose to have an affair with one of her
18-year-old students. In a family, the price of being different may
also be very painful. Sometimes the individual is faced with the
choice between himself and his family. It may be that the only
way he can realize his own potential is by leaving the family. On
the other hand, if the family does allow for difference within
itself, it will be a possible source of enrichment because it is only
in difference that human potential can be fully exploited.

At times some people try to hide certain differences by keeping
certain things secret.

Secrets

Although we have previously devoted a section to 'Secrets' in the
chapter on the royal family (pp. 96–101), we feel the whole area to
be so important for family life that we are taking another opportunity to explore different kinds of secrets. We saw how a secret
of great magnitude led to the destruction of a whole family. But
secrets serve other purposes. They can be a protective device
against self-damage. An example of this might be the homosexual
son who leaves home rather than share his private sexual behaviour with his family. By leaving the home and pursuing his
sexual activities he may actually be preserving his identity. But
as a general rule, the possession of a secret by any member of a
family or members of a family leads to some degree of alienation
or pain. What are the different kinds of secrets that are possible?
First, there is a secret which one person has for himself. An

example of this is Biff in *Death of a Salesman*. Towards the end of the play, in the scene quoted on pp. 148–9, he attempts to bring some truth into the family.

It is possible to equate, like Biff does, secrets with lying. But what a secret means is that in order to maintain it, one often must lie. Carl Jung said of this kind of secret (1954 edn):

> A merely private secret has a destructive effect . . . acts as a burden of guilt . . . cuts off communication . . . isolates . . . (the secret is repressed). We conceal it even from ourselves . . . puts off the unconscious as an independent complex, separates from the unconscious. . . . The complex is thus an autonomous portion of the psyche [which] develops a peculiar fantasy of life of its own.

The second type of secret is the one between two members of a family. This is a secret pact which excludes everyone else and has the effect of creating a special relationship between the two involved which might be incomprehensible to the others. We have this kind of secret between Biff and Willy, when the son finds out his father has a mistress and has been carrying on a cheap affair in second-class hotels with a woman from one of his client's offices. This began as Willy's private secret which Biff discovered by accident:

WILLY (*after a pause*) Well, better get going. I want to get to the school first thing in the morning. Get my suits out of the closet. I'll get my valise. (*Biff doesn't move.*) What's the matter? (*Biff remains motionless, tears falling.*) She's a buyer. Buys for J. H. Simmons. She lives down the hall – they're painting. You don't imagine – (*He breaks off after a pause.*) Now listen pal, she's just a buyer. She sees merchandise in her room and they have to keep it looking just so . . . you mustn't over-emphasize a thing like this. I'll see Birnbaum first thing in the morning.

BIFF Never mind.

WILLY (*getting down beside Biff*) Never mind! He's going to give you those points. I'll see to it.

BIFF He wouldn't listen to you.

151

WILLY   He certainly will listen to me. You need those points
  for the University of Virginia.
BIFF   I'm not going there.
WILLY   Heh? If I can't get him to change that mark, you'll
  make it up in summer school. You've got all summer, to –
BIFF (*his weeping breaking from him*)   Dad. . . .
WILLY (*infected by it*)   Oh my boy. . . .
BIFF   Dad. . . .
WILLY   She's nothing to me, Biff, I was lonely, I was
  terribly lonely.
BIFF   You – you gave her Mama's stockings! (*His tears
  break through and he rises to go.*)
WILLY (*grabbing for Biff*)   I gave you an order!
BIFF   Don't touch me, you – liar!
WILLY   Apologize for that!
BIFF   You fake! You phoney little fake! You fake!

(pp. 94–5)

Until this point Biff has idolized his father. The effect this
revelation has on Biff is two-fold. For the first time, he is forced
to recognize that his father is weak and dishonest. And the effects
of this in his own life are far-reaching and destructive. In effect
Biff punishes himself to spite his father. He refuses to go to
college and embarks on his reckless travels. Not only Biff but the
whole family pays a heavy price for a secret which is shared by
only two people. There is no way for anyone else to rationalize
Biff's subsequent behaviour. The lie lasts fifteen years. An outsider, Bernard attempts to find out what happened that summer.
He asks Willy:

BERNARD   What happened in Boston, Willy? (*Willy looks at
  him as an intruder.*) I just bring it up because you asked me.
WILLY (*angrily*)   Nothing. What do you mean 'What
  happened?' What's that got to do with anything?
BERNARD   Well don't get sore.
WILLY   What are you trying to do, blame it on me? If a boy
  lays down, is that my fault?
BERNARD   Now, Willy, don't get –
WILLY   Well don't – don't talk to me that way! What does
  that mean, 'What happened?'

(p. 74)

What this means for Biff is that many of the problems which can be traced to that very summer are laid upon his head. In effect, he becomes the scapegoat. The Loman family is rich in secrets. To demonstrate yet a third kind, there is the completely open secret, known by all but shared only among Linda, Biff and Happy. This concerns Willy's suicide attempt. When there is such an open secret in the family, all the people involved are forced to behave in devious ways in order to maintain the secret. Linda tells the boys about her dilemma:

LINDA   He's dying, Biff. (*Happy turns quickly to her, shocked.*)
BIFF (*after a pause*)   Why is he dying?
LINDA   He's been trying to kill himself.
BIFF (*with great horror*)   How?
LINDA   I live from day to day.
BIFF   What're you talking about?
LINDA   Remember I wrote you that he had smashed up the car again? In February?
BIFF   Well?
LINDA   The insurance inspector came. He said that they have evidence. That all these accidents in the last year weren't – weren't accidents.
HAPPY   How can they tell that? That's a lie.
LINDA   It seems there's a woman. . . . (*She takes a breath as. . . .*) It seems she was walking down the road and saw his car. She says he wasn't driving fast at all and he didn't skid. She says he came to that little bridge, and then deliberately smashed into the railing, and it was only the shallowness of the water that saved him.
BIFF   Oh, no, he probably just fell asleep again.
LINDA   I don't think he fell asleep.
BIFF   Why not?
LINDA   Last month . . . I was looking for a fuse. The lights blew out, and I went down in the cellar. And behind the fuse-box – it happened to fall out – was a length of rubber pipe – just short.
HAPPY   No kidding?
LINDA   There's a little attachment on the end of it. I knew right away. And sure enough on the bottom of the water heater there's a new little nipple on the gas pipe.

LFS

HAPPY (*angrily*) That – jerk.

BIFF Did you have it taken off?

LINDA I'm – I'm ashamed to. How can I mention it to him? Every day I go down and take away that little rubber pipe. But, when he comes home, I put it back where it was. How can I insult him that way? I don't know what to do.

(pp. 46–7)

In examining the Loman family from this point of view, we might consider it a miracle that they have survived so long as a family, when their relationships are so splintered and fragmented by the preservation of so many secrets. Only by pretence, deceit and lies, is the family able to maintain the myth of perfection (see the royal family, chapter 2). We thought it would be valuable to examine secrets about another kind of family at another point in time. The problem that the therapist faces with the family that has secrets, is that everyone is really scared by what might happen if their secrets become public. People imagine that the worst will happen if they say what they think or feel. This fear is dramatically realized in Ibsen's play *The Wild Duck*. Here we see a family secret being exposed and, as a consequence, a 14-year-old child commits suicide. What we have to bear in mind in this play is that it took place in another time and another social milieu. Not only are the specific issues which are involved with the secret less explosive for us today, but also the social roles are very different. In Ibsen's day, roles were much more rigid and much more clearly defined. The role of the woman, for example, was to stay at home, bear children and be a loyal wife. She was clearly defined as being the weaker sex. Because of this the social rules governing relationships between men and women were sharply prescribed and highly ritualized (at least on a public level). If any of the rules were seen to be violated, public disapproval would be immediate. It is against this background that *The Wild Duck* is set. When we read Ibsen today, it is difficult to understand the strong reaction by the critics and the public. It was an ambivalent reaction. His critics were legion and brutal.

Today, we cannot forget the part that Ibsen played as a social reformer. He challenged some of the most cherished institutions of his time and was hated for it. We have an impression of what London newspaper critics thought of Ibsen's work when it was produced there. Michael Meyer, in his work on Henrik Ibsen, quotes the following from contemporary newspapers:

> From the *Daily Telegraph* on the play *Ghosts*: 'An open drain; a loathsome sore unbandaged; a dirty act done in public: candid foulness.'
> The *Morning Post* labelled Mr Ibsen's plays as: 'sensuality . . . irreverent . . . unwholesome . . . simply blasphemous.'
> The *Victoria World* (writing about *Hedda Gabler*) said the play contained 'hideous nightmares of pessimism. The play is simply a bad escape of moral sewage-gas. . . . Hedda's soul is simply acrawl with the foulest passions of humanity.'

The Ibsen family consists of grandfather, husband and wife and teenage daughter. It is obviously a happy family when the play opens. The first crisis in the family system is precipitated by an outsider, an old school friend of the father, Hjalmar. The friend Gregers tells Hjalmar that his wife has slept with someone else just prior to their marriage. Hjalmar confronts his wife with this information and she takes a risk and tells him it is true:

HJALMAR   Is it true. . . . Can it possibly be true – that there was anything between you and old Mr Werle when you were in service there? (*Clasping his hands*.) And this is the mother of my child! How could you conceal such a thing from me?

GINA   It was wrong of me, I know. I ought to have told you about it long ago.

HJALMAR   You ought to have told me from the very first – then I should have known what sort of woman you were.

GINA   But would you have married me, all the same?

HJALMAR   How can you imagine such a thing!

GINA   No; and that's why I didn't dare tell you anything then. I had got to love you so dearly, as you know. And I couldn't make myself utterly wretched –

Hjalmar's suspicions fall now upon his daughter. Is she his child or not?

HJALMAR   You shall answer this question. Does Hedvig belong to me – or to – ? Well?

GINA (*looking at him with cold bravado*)   I don't know.

HJALMAR (*in a trembling voice*) You don't know?

GINA How should I know? A woman like me –

HJALMAR (*quietly as he turns away from her*) Then I have no longer any part in this house.

GREGERS Think well what you are doing, Hjalmar!

HJALMAR (*putting on his overcoat*) There is nothing here for a man like me to think about.

GREGERS Indeed there is a tremendous lot here for you to think about. You must be something if you are going to reach the goal of self-sacrifice and forgiveness.

HJALMAR I have no desire for that. Never! Never! My hat! (*Takes his hat.*) My home has fallen in ruins around me. (*Bursts into tears.*) I have no child now.

(pp. 144–5)

After her father has stormed out, Hedvig faces Gregers and attempts to find out what the family quarrel was about.

HEDVIG (*sitting upright and wiping away her tears*) Now you must tell me what is the matter. Why won't father have anything more to do with me any more?

GREGERS You mustn't ask that until you are a big girl and grown up.

HEDVIG (*gulping down her tears*) But I can't go on being so utterly miserable until I am a big girl and grown up. I believe I know what it is – perhaps I'm not really father's child.

(pp. 145–6)

Once again we can see how an apparent closed secret has become half-guessed by a child in the family. Once the secret becomes open in the family often what happens is that temporarily feelings change drastically between family members. This is what happens in *The Wild Duck*. Hjalmar, in a fit of righteous indignation, apparently rejects his daughter out of hand. Picking up on an idea given to her by Gregers, she hopes to win back her father's love by making a great sacrifice and shooting the wild duck. Instead, she shoots herself. After this, Hjalmar desperately wants everyone to know that he always loved her:

HJALMAR (*springing up*) Yes, yes. She must live! Oh for God's sake, Relling – just for a moment – just long enough for

me to let her know how overwhelmingly I have loved her
all the time!

RELLING   The heart has been hit. Internal haemorrhage. She
died on the spot.

(p. 162)

In Ibsen's time, any violation of social convention was met by
a standard response, compounded by indignation, contempt and
righteous anger. Here, Hjalmar, too late, is trying to explain that
he really didn't mean what he said. The great fear of many
therapists when they begin their profession is that suicide or
psychosis will result if the therapist provokes the family into
sharing secrets. By refusing to act because of this fear, the therapist is reinforcing the pathology of the family. This is because he
has fallen victim to the same fear that generated the secrets in the
first place. If the secrets are shared, the therapist, like the family,
stands a fighting chance of helping the family survive.

Fantasy

Fantasy is vital. Every person should have this as a part of their
life. It need only be destructive if it is undisciplined and uncontrolled. There is a world of difference between fiction writers who
create strange, bizarre worlds within their books and 'schizophrenics' who may create similar worlds but use them to retreat
from reality. Our lives are filled with fantasy. We only have to
consider the advertising media to see this very clearly. They are
based on the 'if only' myth. If only we use this soap or drink this
beer or smoke this cigarette or try this service, almost immediately
we are led to believe we will become much more desirable, or
much more masculine or even end up with a new girl-friend or
husband or wife. In setting out to create a demand for a new
product, the media deliberately aim at our most secret desires.
The late Walt Disney realised this secret. He created a new world
of fantasy in central Florida, 20 miles south-west of Orlando.
Here a 400 million dollar, 27,500 acre enclave called Walt Disney
World was opened to the public. *Time* magazine reporting on the
new Fantasy Land, 18 October 1971, stated that 'the latest Disney
enterprise, 4 years in the building, includes a spotlessly clean

157

amusement area, 2 enormous and elaborate hotels with Marinas and beaches, 2 championship calibre golf courses, lavishly landscaped lakes and futuristic transportation network linking everything'. The creators of this dream-come-true have provided hotels, shops, beaches and other recreational facilities for those who can afford it. *Time* goes on to say that 'Disneymen call their creation a "Total Destination Resort." Not just a stop-over, in other words, but a place to spend a weekend or a week. Early guests have been staying at the Polynesian Village Hotel built in Tahitian-style along the lake shore with 500 rooms in 5 so-called "long houses".'

As the business empires use fantasy to maintain their economic survival, individual persons may use it to enrich their lives. Lawrence Durrell, in his work *The Alexandria Quartet* speaks of this point. Two of his characters in the book, Clea the artist and Darley the schoolmaster, have just completed making love. They are talking about it (1970 edn, p. 728):

'Did you ever imagine this?'
'We must both have done. Otherwise it would not have happened.'

Durrell here is pointing out the idea that in order for something to happen, it at least must fall into the realm of possibility before it can really happen. Fantasy, however, has a double-edged power. On the one hand, it is the means by which we can realize our potential. On the other hand, it can be used to hide ourselves away and to protect ourselves from the things we are afraid of. This latter is the way that the men in the Loman family use their fantasy. Willie tries to hide the reality of his failure as a salesman from his two young sons and his friends:

WILLY   Don't say? Tell you a secret, boys. Don't breathe it to a soul. Someday I'll have my own business, and I'll never have to leave home anymore.
HAPPY   Like Uncle Charley, heh?
WILLY   Bigger than Uncle Charley's! Because Charley is not – liked. He's liked, but he's not – well-liked.
BIFF   Where'd you go this time, Dad?
WILLY   Well, I got on the road and went north to Providence. Met the Mayor.

BIFF The Mayor of Providence!

WILLY He was sitting in the hotel lobby.

BIFF What did he say?

WILLY He said 'Morning!' and I said 'You got a fine city
here, Mayor.' And then he had coffee with me. And then
I went to Waterbury. . . . You and Hap and I, and I'll
show you all the towns. America is full of beautiful towns
and fine, upstanding people. And they know me, boys,
they know me up and down New England. The finest
people. And when I bring you fellows up, there'll be open
sesame for all of us. 'Cause one thing boys; I have friends.
I can park my car in any street in New England and the
cops protect it like their own! This summer, heh?

(pp. 23-4)

Willy's formula for success is based on fantasy. When discussing
his work with his family, we can see this very clearly:

WILLY . . . because the man who makes an appearance in
the business world, the man who creates personal interest,
is the man who gets ahead. Be liked and you will never
want. Take me, for instance. I never have to wait in line
to see a buyer. 'Willy Loman is here!' That's all they have
to know and I go right through.

BIFF Did you knock them dead, Pop?

WILLY Knocked 'em cold in Providence, slaughtered them
in Boston.

(pp. 25-6)

The fantasy which he is trying to project to his children is
almost completely destroyed when he is talking to his wife Linda
about the money he has made:

LINDA . . . Did you sell anything?

WILLY I did five hundred gross in Providence and seven
hundred gross in Boston.

LINDA No! Wait a minute, I've got a pencil. (*She pulls the
pencil and paper out of her apron.*) That makes your
commission . . . two hundred – My God! two hundred
and twelve dollars!

WILLY Well, I didn't figure it yet but. . . .

LINDA How much did you do?

159

WILLY Well, I – I did about a hundred and eighty gross in
Providence. Well, no, it came to roughly two hundred
gross on the whole trip.

LINDA (*without hesitation*) Two hundred gross. That's . . .
(*She figures.*)

WILLY The trouble was that three of the stores were half-
closed for inventory in Boston. Otherwise I woulda broke
records.

LINDA Well it makes seventy dollars and some pennies.
That's very good.

(p. 27)

Willy simply cannot face the reality of not being a top salesman.
He prefers a dream world. It is far more attractive. One way to
deal with a painful experience is to retreat into fantasy and dream
of what might have happened 'if only'. Fantasy can be a great
destructive force in relationships if we refuse to accept a person
as they are and insist on trying to make them fit our image. An
example can be found in *The Glass Menagerie* by Tennessee
Williams. In the scene between mother and daughter, it is evening
and the mother, Amanda, and the daughter, Laura, are waiting
the arrival of a young man for dinner:

AMANDA No dear, you go in front and study your typewriter
chart. Practice your shorthand a little. Stay fresh and
pretty! – It's almost time for our gentleman caller to start
arriving.
(*She flounces girlishly toward the kitchenette.*)
How many do you suppose we are going to entertain this
afternoon?
(*Tom throws down the paper and jumps up with a groan.*)

LAURA (*alone in the dining room*) I don't believe we are going
to receive any, mother.

AMANDA (*re-appearing airily*) What! not one? You must be joking!
(*Laura nervously echoes her laugh. She slips in a fugitive manner
through the half-open portières and draws them in gently behind
her. A shaft of very clear light is thrown on her face against the
faded tapestry of the curtains.*)
(*Music – the Glass Menagerie, faintly, lightly.*)
Not one gentleman caller? It can't be true. There must be
a flood – There must have been a tornado!

LAURA   It isn't a flood, it's not a tornado mother, I'm just
   not popular like you were in Blue Mountain. . . .
(*Tom utters another groan. Laura glances at him with a faint,
apologetic smile. Her voice catching a little.*)
LAURA   Mother's afraid I'm going to be an old maid.
(*The scene dims out with Glass Menagerie music.*)

(pp. 239–40)

The tragedy of the scene becomes realized when we see that
the daughter is a cripple. All through the play, the mother refuses
to acknowledge this disability. Amanda and Laura are talking
about Laura's chances of finding a young man:

AMANDA   Girls not cut-out for business careers usually wind
   up married to some nice man. (*Gets up with a spark of
   revival.*) Sister, that's what you'll do!
(*Laura utters a startled, doubtful laugh. She reaches quickly for
a piece of glass.*)
LAURA   But mother –
AMANDA   Yes?
(*Crossing to photograph.*)
LAURA (*in a tone of frightened apology*)   I'm – crippled!
AMANDA   Nonsense! Laura, I have told you never, never to
   use that word. Why, you're not crippled, you just have a
   little defect – hardly noticeable, even! When people have
   some slight disadvantage like that, they cultivate other
   things to make up for it – develop charm and vivacity –
   and – charm! That's all you have to do! (*She turns again
   to the photograph.*) One thing your father had plenty of was
   charm!
(*Tom motions to the fiddle in the wings. The scene fades out with
music.*)

(pp. 246–7)

In both of the above examples, we see people retreating into
fantasy as a way of denying a present situation. In Ibsen's *Wild
Duck*, Hjalmar Ekdal is already dreaming of the future and how
one day he will be the saviour of his family. His father has been
dishonoured and Ekdal hopes to save the family name by inventing
something which will revolutionize photography:

HJALMAR   I vowed to myself that if I devoted my powers to
this trade, I would so dignify it that it would become both
an art and a science. And so I decided to make this
remarkable invention.

GREGERS   And what is the nature of the invention? What is
the idea?

HJALMAR   My dear fellow, you must not ask me for details
yet. It takes time, you know. And you mustn't suppose
that it is vanity that impels me. I assure you I don't work
for my own sake. No, no; it is the object of my life that
is in my thoughts night and day.

GREGERS   What object is that?

HJALMAR   Have you forgotten that poor, old white-haired man?

GREGERS   Your poor father? Yes, but what exactly can you do
for him?

HJALMAR   I can revive his dead self-respect by restoring the
name of Ekdal to honour and dignity.

GREGERS   So that is the object of your life.

(p. 119)

Ekdal is using fantasy to project himself into the role of the
family saviour. Later, the same fantasy serves a different purpose.
Ekdal tries to ensure his daughter's prospects by excusing his
present poverty and looking to the wealth of the future:

HJALMAR (*with emotion*)   My child! Yes! My child, first and
foremost. Come to me, Hedvig. (*Stroking her hair*.) What
day is it tomorrow?

HEDVIG   No, you mustn't say anything about it, father.

HJALMAR   It makes my heart bleed to think what a meagre
affair it will be. Just a little festive gathering in the attic
there –

HEDVIG   But that will be just lovely, father!

RELLING   You wait until the great invention is finished,
Hedvig!

HJALMAR   Yes, indeed – Then you will see me, Hedvig. I am
determined to make your future safe. You shall live in
comfort all your life. I shall demand something for you –
something or other; and that shall be the poor inventor's
only reward.

(pp. 124–5)

For the family the fantasy serves yet another function. Hjalmar is lazy and does very little work but as long as the myth of the invention is preserved, his 'idle role' is legitimized. In this way, the family maintains its balance until the stress becomes too great and this is no longer possible. Every person needs to be stimulated and to have his needs fulfilled. The greater the deprivation, the larger the part fantasy comes to play in our lives. The Black Box experiments which have been explored in America inevitably result in some kind of breakdown in the individual. Either he cracks up or begs to be let out. Colin Wilson, in his recent book *New Pathways in Psychology* (1972), writes about this phenomenon (p. 201):

> Confinement in the Black Room can produce nervous breakdown in most people within a matter of days and intelligent people tend to crack more quickly than stupid ones, no doubt because they worry more. . . . It is no doubt true that Einstein could stand the Black Room longer than James Bond, but not indefinitely longer. And yet the Black Room should not drive human beings insane; there was no actual hardship. They are not threatened with suffocation or starvation. What rises up against them in the Black Room is their own immaturity, their own weaknesses. The general solution would be to produce a type of human being capable of self-sustaining mental activity, a mental activity so firmly grounded in the sense of objective values that it could not be eroded by the usual fears, day-dreams, confusions.

In a family where the relationships are open and satisfying, fantasy is not a private affair – it may be openly discussed without fear of retribution. Furthermore, in this situation, the fantasy may even be acted on and prove to be a stimulant to growth and a possible new experience. In *The Wild Duck*, we see how this idea of make-believe is used. Gregers and Relling are discussing the idea of make-believe:

GREGERS   And what treatment are you using for Hjalmar?
RELLING   My usual one. I'm trying to keep up the make-believe of life in him.
GREGERS   The make-believe? I don't think I heard you correctly?

RELLING   Yes, I said make-believe. That is the stimulating
principle of life, you know.

(p. 151)

Fantasy takes many forms. If it gets out of control it can be
destructive, sometimes even resulting in our having a completely
unreal image of someone who is close to us.

The model child

'MODEL' SON GETS LIFE FOR STABBING

A 19-year-old Boys' Brigade bandsman, was regarded by his
parents as being a 'model' son and was described by his
teachers as a very kind, courteous and gentle boy. Yet he took
a cut-throat razor and a six inch dagger to a football match
and stabbed a total stranger to death in the street right
afterwards.

(*Evening Standard*, 20 July 1972.)

In 1924 in a famous Chicago case, two wealthy, bright, attractive
teenagers killed a 14-year-old boy for no apparent reason and with
whom they were barely acquainted. Richard Loeb and Nathan
Leopold both came from upper-class families and were generally
regarded as intelligent and well behaved. This act of murder was
so inexplicable that for the first time in American legal history,
alienists (as psychiatrists were then known) were called in to
examine the defendants. Major MacCormack, a newspaper publisher and friend of the families, went so far as to beg Freud to
psychoanalyse the two boys. William Randolph Hearst, hearing
that Freud was ill, was prepared to charter a special liner so that
Freud could travel undisturbed by other company. Freud declined both offers (Jones, 1957, p. 103; quoted in Menninger,
1966.) After a brilliant defence by the famous attorney Clarence
Darrow, the boys received life imprisonment.

Every professional who works with families has at some time or
another heard the words 'he was a model child'. Yet time and again
the same child will be labelled as mentally ill, become delinquent
or even a murderer. In the two cases we have cited there is the
paradox that the child viewed by parents, teachers and friends as

being obedient, responsible, trustworthy and in fact almost a perfect child, can dramatically become a monster.

The three worlds of the model child

Every child lives in many worlds. Each world has its own rules; first, there is the family, a primary influence; next, there is the powerful peer group which may sometimes even be in direct contradiction to the family; finally, there is the world of the child himself where all influences must meet and be balanced, and where eventually he must face himself.

Each of these worlds may be separate and distinct. To his family and his friends, he may represent totally different images. The myth of the model child is a possible result of this balancing act. In this kind of situation, it is almost as if the child leads a secret life away from his family. While the family is extolling his virtues, he may for example be involved in stealing, cruelty to animals and the kind of sexual adventures which would shock his parents.

Of equal interest is the kind of child whose behaviour in all spheres is reputed to be a model of goodness until suddenly he becomes involved in an act or series of acts which shocks his family or the community. It is often at this point that the family first becomes involved in therapy. In the Loman family, exactly this kind of situation was precipitated by the Boston episode. Until this point, Biff might have been called a model child. After this, his behaviour radically changes. We have already seen what happens to the family in some detail up until this point and until Willy's suicide. However, what we would like to explore is what might have happened in therapy if the family had sought therapy at this point. This is pure licence on our part, for of course we would never know how the family would behave. What we will use the section for is to explore the communication model by Satir, Jackson and Haley, and also review the way the Loman family communicates among itself. The Loman family have arrived and are being introduced:

THERAPIST   Is everybody comfortable? Good. Will someone say whose idea it was to come here?

WILLY   It was my idea. I make the decisions in this family.

THERAPIST   Let me check that out. I would like everyone to speak for themselves. Tell me, Linda, whose idea do you think it was to come here?

LINDA   It was Willy's idea but, of course, I thought it a good idea.

THERAPIST   Good. Happy, what was your idea about coming here?

HAPPY   Well, Pop told us we were coming.

THERAPIST   And do you always do what Pop tells you to do?

WILLY   They're good boys, they're the best.

THERAPIST   I have a special way of working with families. I do like everyone to speak for themselves. Could you answer my question, Happy?

HAPPY   Sometimes. (*Laughing.*) Not always.

THERAPIST   OK. Biff, let me ask you. What was your idea about coming here?

BIFF   I don't know what we're doing here. Everything is OK to me.

THERAPIST   Let me see now. Some people feel it is important to be here, others feel that they are not sure. It is important to allow for differences in a family. Let me find out what some of the problems are in the family. Let me start with you, Willy.

WILLY   There's a problem. (*Pointing at Biff.*) He won't go to summer school. He's been acting pretty strange lately. He won't do what he is told. He won't listen to me.

THERAPIST   Let me see, let me ask Biff.

BIFF   Why should I listen to him. I don't trust him.

LINDA   Oh Biff, how can you say such a thing to your father. He loves you.

THERAPIST   How we show affection and love to others is important. In this family, Willy, how do you show Biff that you love him?

BIFF   He doesn't love anybody but himself.

THERAPIST   What you are saying may be important. However I would like to hear what Willy has to say.

WILLY   Love that boy! I slaved all my life for him, to make things possible for him. With my help he's going to be great! All he has to do is to go to summer school, the world is at his feet. He's a Loman.

THERAPIST   Let me see. You're saying you show your love for Biff by working hard and supporting him. Biff, what do you think about that and how do you show your love and affection for your father?

BIFF   He's a phoney! If you only knew (*stops.*)

THERAPIST   If I only knew what?

BIFF   I can't say.

THERAPIST   What will happen if you say?

BIFF   Nothing. I didn't mean anything.

THERAPIST   That's not clear to me. I'm not sure if it is clear to the family. On the one hand you're saying that Willy is a phoney. On the other hand, you are saying that it doesn't mean anything to you. Is it a rule in this family that you do not talk clearly to each other?

WILLY   No, us Lomans always speak our minds.

THERAPIST   Good. Let me see if that is actually the case. Biff, what did you mean when you said your father was a phoney?

BIFF   Just that. He is. He says one thing and does another. You can't trust him.

THERAPIST   That's not clear either. Maybe I could ask Willy to clear it up.

WILLY (*blustering*)   What do you mean, ask me? I don't know what he is talking about. Why don't you ask him why he flunked Math. Three universities wanted to give him a scholarship. He messed it up.

THERAPIST   Schooling seems to be an important part in this family. Willy, how did you let Biff know that school was important?

WILLY   But I tell him all the time. Biff, I say, you gonna do great things.

THERAPIST   Yes, but how do you actually show Biff that school is important?

WILLY   After he flunked Math, I said I would go and see his teacher and maybe arrange special classes. So what does he say? 'Don't bother, don't go.' That's what he said!

THERAPIST   I would like Biff to speak for himself.

BIFF   That's right. I told him not to go. I don't trust him anymore.

THERAPIST   When did you lose your trust in your father?

167

BIFF   Why don't you ask him?

THERAPIST   I'm asking you.

BIFF   Why don't you ask him what he does on his trips to Boston, for example?

LINDA   What, do you mean –

WILLY   Don't listen to him!

THERAPIST   Is this a secret in the family? You know, all families have secrets. Some small, some big.

WILLY   There are no secrets in my family!

BIFF   Hah!

THERAPIST   What will happen in this family if the secret is shared? Maybe we could talk a bit about this now and then pick it up again next time.

The secret of what happened in Boston in the Loman family is the precipitating factor, the cancer that eats away at the relationships and ultimately helps destroy a member of the family. The above imaginary episode gives some small insight into what might have taken place. If therapy had been successful one might have worked with the following family areas: allowing for differences, sharing of secrets, allowing for weaknesses, and the removal of fantasy. In this way the salesman could have retained his integrity. There would have been no need for a destructive fantasy and there would have been no need for anyone to fall victim to an unfulfilled desire.

5 THE ALBEE FAMILY

A Delicate Balance by Edward Albee

List of characters

Agnes	A handsome woman in her late fifties.
Tobias	Her husband. A few years older.
Claire	Agnes's sister, several years younger.
Julia	Agnes and Tobias's daughter, 36 years. (Angular.)
Edna and Harry	Very much like Agnes and Tobias.

Synopsis of the plot of the play

Claire lives with Tobias and Agnes. She is alcoholic. At the beginning of the play, we learn of the two facts that are to trigger off all the succeeding events. Julia is on her way home and Harry and Edna arrive.

Harry and Edna are scared. They have faced the essential emptiness and meaninglessness of their lives and have been so frightened they felt the need to run to their best friends' house for company. They decided to stay for a time.

Julia's arrival explodes an already delicate situation. Her spoiled childish behaviour sets up a series of rows between all the people in the house. The events are likened to a plague and Harry and Edna are accused of being the carriers.

But it is Tobias who finally has to face himself; in a self-tortured climax, he tells Harry that he both wants them to leave and to stay. Harry and Edna leave and the Albee family are left, so early in the morning, to face what remains of their relationships.

The tortured family

The Albee family is characterized by loneliness and alienation. Husband and wife have somehow lost any essential contact they might have once had. Their lives are uneventful, uninspiring – and probably boring and stultifying. They do not even sleep together, and have to use Agnes's alcoholic sister as a third person to keep away the loneliness that so frightens their best friends. They have everything: they are fairly wealthy, healthy and wise Americans, with few external problems and yet their lives are terribly unsatisfying. None of the Albee family are capable of taking a real stand to the down-hill momentum of their lives. And thus, when faced with an essential crisis that requires strength and decision, no one can act with real determination. Tobias tries to but his finest attempt results in his being almost completely torn down the middle.

The Albee family represents a whole facet of the twentieth century. We live in a society whose social organization is geared to a way of life whose central demand is material survival. The central demand has long departed, yet somehow we have failed to adapt to the new world. We have not created new values to replace the old. The great danger is that we do not out-reach ourselves, that our moral muscles become slack from too few environmental demands. The Albee family has drifted so far down on the sea of material comfort and avoidance of moral discomfort that when a real challenge emerges, no one is fit enough to accept it. Instead of a battle and victory, we have battle and resignation. We are left as we were before, little has altered. Life will continue its faltering way.

The Albee family helps us to look at four major areas of family life. Decision-making and survival are two closely linked themes, which we deal with separately here, though their relationship is obvious. Also closely linked with the idea of survival is the idea of flexibility; in some deeply troubled families individuals become 'locked' into highly predictable roles. This constitutes our third area of analysis. But we open our discussion by looking at pain.

Pain

Suffering and hurt begin with birth. Pain is part of being alive. Each contact with another person brings about the possibilities of pleasure or pain or both. Pain is big business.[1] The huge pharmaceutical companies, hospitals, doctors, psychiatrists, all are devoted to producing comfort for the mind and body. Once, it was the Churches' responsibility alone to comfort the troubled soul. Today, there is a whole new priesthood. The new salvation is offered by the therapists, the psychiatrists, and spearheaded by such radical groups as Gestalt, encounter, meditation, drugs (and family therapists). Equally fascinating is the idea that pain is abnormal. An equally large industry is devoted to the creation of the 'happiness myth', if we accept the idea that life naturally must be beautiful. The American Dream was the product of such thinking. A country where everyone is happy, wealthy and free. But Utopian dreams always crumble in the face of reality. When this happens and the pain comes, we find ourselves ill-equipped to deal with it. We can attempt to understand pain from two angles; pain that is self-imposed and pain that is imposed by others. In the first category we might consider such experiences as inadequacy and failure in the whole period of adolescence. Pain inspired by others might involve rejection and humiliation. The most typical response to this is stoicism and denial at least in public. Pain is a private affair which is usually not shared except in very special relationships. We only seek professional help when the pain becomes unbearable and interferes with our everyday activities. The family is no exception. When one member feels hurt, the pain affects everyone. Such pain is inevitable. The question is how to come to terms with it. Suffering can be handled in a number of ways, some constructive and some destructive. The individual might become depressed, alcoholic, suicidal. He might simply maintain a mute silence or internalize his anger, outwardly remaining calm. The alternative is to use pain as a growing experience. If we see pain as a distress signal and share this suffering with others close to us, we are offering ourselves and them a chance to grow and find new ways of satisfying our needs. The healthy person, too, knows pain in his relationships. If a person is sensitive, he will know that part of the price he must pay for establishing a relationship is the possibility of pain. Everyone gets rejected at some time. There is also the problem of adjusting to differentness which, at times, can be difficult. With a healthy person who possibly feels insecure or doesn't think he has much value, these potential problems may seem insurmountable. To him, the possibility of pain is far greater either because he does not learn from his past experiences or because pain is the only meaningful way he has of relating to other people. Without exception all members of the Albee family are poorly integrated. For a variety of reasons they lie, cheat, deceive and deny, with the result that the relationships are barren, alienated and poverty-stricken. Tobias and Agnes have not slept together for many years. This emerges when, by force of circumstances, they are forced to spend the night together. Tobias and Agnes are discussing the previous night's experience:

AGNES So odd.

TOBIAS Hm.

AGNES There was a stranger in my room last night.

TOBIAS Who?

AGNES You.

TOBIAS Ah.

AGNES It was nice to have you there.

TOBIAS (*slight smile*) Hm.

AGNES *Le temps perdu.* I've never understood that; 'perdu' means lost, not merely . . . past, but it was nice to have you there, though I remember when it was a constancy, how easily I would fall asleep, pace my breathing to your breathing, and if we were touching! ah, what a splendid cocoon that was. But last night – what a shame, what sadness – you were a stranger, and I stayed awake.

TOBIAS *I'm* sorry.

AGNES Were you asleep at all?

TOBIAS No.

AGNES I would go half, then awake – your unfamiliar presence, sir, I *could* get used to it again. . . . And I was awake when you left my room again.

TOBIAS (*gentle reproach*) You could have said.

AGNES (*curious at the truth*) I felt shy.

TOBIAS (*pleased surprise*) Hm!

(pp. 81–2)

This is a very touching moment. Agnes and Tobias are sharing something precious and loving. But somehow Agnes cannot handle this feeling, she cannot enjoy it. She must spoil it by deliberately introducing the topic of her sister Claire, revealing her jealousy:

AGNES   Did you go to Claire?

TOBIAS   I never go to Claire.

AGNES   Did you go to Claire to talk?

TOBIAS   I never go to Claire.

AGNES   We must always envy someone we should not, be jealous of those who have so much less. You and Claire make so much sense together, talk so well.

TOBIAS   I never go to Claire at night, or talk with her alone – save publicly.

AGNES (*small smile*)   In public rooms. . . . Like this.

TOBIAS   Yes.

AGNES   Have *never*.

TOBIAS   Please?

AGNES   Do we dis*like* happiness? We manufacture such a portion of our own despair . . . such busy folk.

(pp. 82–3)

It is not unreasonable to assume from this passage that Agnes suspects her sister and Tobias of having a sexual relationship. This would go some way towards accounting for her hostility towards their relationship. For example when Agnes and Tobias are talking towards the beginning of the play, Agnes is very bitter:

AGNES   If I were to list the mountain of my burdens – if I had a thick pad and a month to spare – that bending my shoulders *most*, with the possible exception of Julia's trouble with marriage, would be your – it must be instinctive, I think, or *reflex*, that's more like it, your reflex defense of everything that Claire. . . .

TOBIAS   (*Very nice, but there is steel underneath*)   Stop it Agnes.

AGNES (*a little laugh*)   Are you going to throw something at me? Your glass? My goodness, I hope not . . . that awful anisette all over everything.

TOBIAS (*patient*)   No.

AGNES (*quietly daring him*)   What then?

TOBIAS (*looking at his hand*)   I shall sit very quietly . . .

AGNES   . . . as always. . . .

TOBIAS   . . . yes, and I shall will you to apologize to your
sister for what I must in truth tell you I thought a
most. . . .

AGNES   Apologize! To her? To Claire? I have spent my adult
life apologizing *for* her; I will not double my humiliation
by apologizing *to* her.

(pp. 15–16)

This present hostility seems to be part of an on-going war between
Agnes and Claire. We discover that their conflict goes right back
to their own childhood, and somehow, for some reason, they have
never been able to resolve their differences:

CLAIRE (*a twang in her voice*)   Maw used to say 'Claire
girl' . . . she had an uncle named Claire so she always
called me Claire-girl –

AGNES (*no patience with it*)   That is not so.

CLAIRE   'Claire girl,' she used to say, 'when you go out into
the world, get dumped outa the nest or pushed by your
sister. . . .'

AGNES (*steady but burning*)   Lies. (*Eyes slits.*) She kept you,
allowed you . . . tolerated! Put up with your filth, your . . .
emancipated womanhood. (*To Julia, overly sweet.*) Even in
her teens your Auntie Claire had her own and very special
ways, was very . . . advanced.

CLAIRE (*laughs*)   Had a ball, same as you, 'cept I wasn't puce
with socially proper remorse every time. (*To Julia.*) Your
mommy got her pudenda scuffed a couple of times herself
'fore she met old Toby, you know.

TOBIAS   Your what?

AGNES (*majesty*)   My pudenda.

CLAIRE (*a little grumpy*)   You can come on all forgetful in
your old age, if you want to, but just remember.

AGNES (*quiet anger*)   I am not an old woman. (*Sudden
thought. To Tobias.*) Am I?

(pp. 60–1)

If we look carefully at the triangle of relationships, we see a
great deal of unnecessary and self-imposed pain. If only Agnes
and Tobias were more honest in their relationships then much of

this could have been prevented. This breakdown in sexual relationships between Tobias and Agnes, accompanied by a breakdown in communication, is a fairly typical one in disturbed families. Open discussion about sex between parents is rather rare in most families. Although less true today we still tend to shroud sex with secrecy and enclose it with a social taboo. This may sound surprising to many people but in a recent study published by Arno Karlen (1971) called *Sexuality and Homosexuality* he reports (p. vii): 'The more I read and talk to serious students of the subject, the more convinced I become that what passes for an informed, enlightened view of sex among educated laymen is twenty to fifty years out of date.'

As a result the way we learn about sex is often confusing and fraught with difficulty. Here the role of the family therapist requires courage. He must not be afraid to ask direct questions about the sex relationships even though he knows some of the answers might be painful. He will often meet great resistance from the family. He must press on in the face of stubborn resistance, to accomplish his goal of developing open communication. This is particularly vital in the sexual area because a great deal of pain emanates from this problem as it does in the Albee family.

There is no doubt that Toby gets a great deal out of his relationship with Claire. If we consider the poverty of his relationship with Agnes coupled with the fact that Julia is much closer to her mother, we can realize that without Claire, he might be quite isolated. Despite the comfort it might bring him, this in the long run makes the family situation much worse. It feeds Agnes's jealousy and it increases their estrangement. Julia is a tormented person. At the age of 36 she has had four failed marriages. She still feels great guilt over the death of her younger brother and seems incapable of dealing with crisis situations, reverting back to child-like behaviour. It is as if she must continually return home but needs an excuse to do so. If we look at the communication when she does come home we can get some insight into how this comes about. Julia is given a confused message each time she returns home. Before she arrived, Agnes had told Toby very clearly that she did not want Julia back. However, when Julia does return, no one says anything. This is frank collusion. The message that Julia must be getting is that her behaviour is acceptable and it is OK to return home.

Often people do not realize that they are colluding with behaviour which they dislike. Agnes says that she does not want Julia home, but takes an inordinate interest in all the details of the latest failed marriage – even to the extent of wanting to make a big secret out of it. It is almost as though she enjoys hearing of Julia's problems!

CLAIRE   I have been trying, without very much success, to find out why Miss Julie here is come home.

AGNES   I would imagine Julia is come home because she wishes to be, and it is where she belongs if she wants.

TOBIAS   That's logistics, isn't it?

AGNES   You too?

JULIA   He's against everything!

AGNES   Your father?

JULIA   Doug!

AGNES   You needn't make a circus of it; tell me later, when. . . .

JULIA   War, marriage, money, children. . . .

AGNES   You needn't!

JULIA   You! Daddy! Government! Claire – if he'd met her . . . everything!

CLAIRE   Well, I doubt he'd dislike *me*; I'm against everything too.

AGNES (*to Julia*)   You're tired; we'll talk about it after. . . .

JULIA (*sick, disgust*)   I've talked about it! I just talked about it!

AGNES (*quiet boring in*)   I'm sure there's more.

JULIA   There is no more.

AGNES (*clenched teeth*)   There is a great deal more, and I'll hear it from you later, when we're alone. You have not come to us in your fourth debacle. . . .

JULIA   HE IS OPPOSED! AND THAT IS ALL! TO EVERYTHING!

AGNES (*after a small silence*)   Perhaps after dinner.

JULIA   NO! NOT PERHAPS AFTER DINNER!

TOBIAS   ALL OF YOU! BE STILL!

(*Silence.*)

CLAIRE (*flat; to Tobias*)   Are we having our dividend or are we not? (*Silence: then, a gentle mocking apology.*) All happy families are alike.

(pp. 54–5)

Pain in a family is in every person. But as we can see from the above example, no one is really prepared to be honest about what causes them suffering. And in avoiding the confrontation, the pain becomes worse, and, remaining unchecked, can lead to worse consequences. Pain generates pain. We can see a pattern in the Albee family of avoiding the communication and decisions which would cause pain. This is a very common pattern. What is not always realized is that the avoidance of immediate pain is no guarantee that the suffering will go away or diminish in the future. On the contrary, evidence seems to suggest that such avoidance or denial has its own consequences such as physical illness of a psychological origin. It is likely that the unchecked pain will act as a slow poison in the relationship between the people. It is the responsibility of the therapist to help the family share its pain openly between its members so that eventually everyone can take part in offering warmth and comfort to the others.

Pain is just one thing that can be shared between family members. Decision-making can be another.

Decision-making

Decision-making is part of everyday life. Not only do we have to contend with our own decisions, but frequently the decisions of others have a profound effect on our lives. This is particularly obvious in the political sphere, where the Government makes decisions in the name of the people which affect the whole nation to preserve the illusion that we have direct influence in this kind of decision-making. But it is often apparent that direct influence by the mass of people is purely nominal. A major international example is the British Government's decision to join the Common Market. This decision sparked off great internal conflicts. The decision seemed inevitable, despite the fact that a great number of people were opposed to such a move. The same thing happened in Denmark. Thus every decision has a price. Though we may gain something, we also may lose something. This is equally true in family life. Whether the decisions are purely personal or directly affect the whole family, every decision means some kind of change. In such a tight-knit system as the family, any change no matter how large or small may ultimately affect the whole family. Of interest to us here is the process of how decisions are made. The kinds of questions that are important for us are: Who shares in the decision-making; Who originated the question; How was the decision finally made; and, How does it affect every member of the family?

Patterns of decision-making vary from family to family, culture to culture. In an English lower-class family for example, the husband might take the part of an absentee authority. Thus power is delegated to the wife to make decisions, but the husband must be kept informed and has the final sanction. This might be different in a comparable family in America, where the woman seems to have more real power and decision-making is more of a shared process. Often, for example, the children are allowed to have a real influence. As a contrast, in Black lower-class families the family might be dominated by the mother, which ties in with the fact that the father spends a great deal of his time away from the family. In addition to cultural differences there are also many different individual styles of decision-making. Patterns are established within each family and these are often transmitted from generation to generation. For example, historically, the husband has taken the role of provider for the family which means he has had control of an important area of finance. In Denmark, for example, it is very common for the wife not to know how much her husband earns. This 'secret' is very important in terms of control by augmenting the husband's power when it comes to making decisions concerning money. The more people involved in a decision, the more complicated it can become. (This has been recognized in industry where numerous courses have been developed with the express purpose of teaching people how to make decisions.) Within the family there are many different kinds of decisions. There is the unilateral decision where the individual concerned makes his decision without consulting anyone. This can lead to all kinds of problems, as King Lear discovered when he decided to share his empire with all his daughters. By doing this it limits the response of the others. It is presented as a *fait accompli*. In a sense, it can be a devaluation of the others. This is a secret decision where the member follows a course of activity without telling anyone in the family. The adolescent does this all the time. The family will only find out much later, if at all.

Another decision-making method is for the parents to share a decision between themselves while deliberately excluding the children. The rationale for this is that the children are too young and do not understand. Goffman calls this yet another sign that children are not quite people. He says (1970, p. 108):

> Action can be forced, but a forced show of feeling is only a show. An affronted recipient can take action against a person who is insufficiently differential but typically must disguise his specific reason for this corrective action. Only children, presumably can be openly sanctioned by the recipient for showing improper difference; this is one sign that we hold children to be not – yet – persons.

There is also the conspiracy decision. Like a plot against the State, this kind of decision takes place in secrecy. It is aimed against one or more members of the family and it involves taking a course of action against them. Where we will often meet this is where a decision is taken that a family member should be hospitalized. Very often the particular member is the last person to hear about it and is faced with his family united against him. When he returns the same thing may happen. A policy decision will have been made in his absence as to how best to treat him. The same kind of conspiracy is very common when a family member is dying. Commenting on this phenomenon, Dr Elisabeth Kubler Ross states (1970, p. 142):

> The dying patient's problems come to an end, but the family's problems go on. Many of these problems can be decreased by discussing them before the death of a family member. The tendency is, unfortunately, to hide the feelings from the patient, to attempt to keep a smiling face and a front of make-believe cheerfulness which has to break down sooner or later. We have interviewed a terminally-ill husband who said, 'I know I have only a short time to live but don't tell my wife, she could not take it.' When we spoke to the visiting wife in a casual encounter, she volunteered almost the same words. She knew and he knew but neither had the courage to share it with the other – and this after 30 years of marriage! There was a young chap who was able to encourage them to share their awareness, while he remained in the

179

room at the patient's request. Both were greatly relieved that they no longer had to play a deceitful game and proceeded to make arrangements which either one alone was unable to do. Later, they were able to smile about their 'childish game', as they themselves called it and were wondering who knew it first and how long it would have taken them without help from outside.

Finally we might have a look at the shared decision. This is both the least common and the most difficult. Ideally, the whole family is involved. Every member is encouraged to speak for himself and make his own contribution. One reason it is so difficult, is that inevitably compromises will have to be made. Every member is encouraged to take risks and, in so doing, he comes to feel himself as a valuable person.

One type of decision that we have not dealt with is the 'decision by default', which is central to the problem of the Albee family. In this family, decisions are not so much made as assumed. Each individual works on the assumption that he knows what the other person wants and so does not bother to check it out. This happened to Tobias and Agnes over whether or not to have another child after their son died. It is many, many years later that they dare talk about this. And even now it takes a crisis before they can approach the subject. It is very early in the morning and Agnes and Tobias have been talking about the events of the previous day. Agnes is blaming her husband for all that goes wrong. Then she introduces the subject of the child they might have had:

AGNES (*remorseless*) When Teddy died? (*Pause.*) We *could* have had another son; we could have tried. But no . . . those months – or was it a year – ?
TOBIAS No more of this!
AGNES . . . I think it was a year, when you spilled yourself on my belly, sir? 'Please? Please Tobias?' No you wouldn't even say it out; I don't want another child, another loss. 'Please? Please Tobias?' And guiding you, *trying* to hold you in?
TOBIAS (*tortured*) Oh Agnes! Please!
AGNES Don't leave me then, like that. Not again, Tobias. Please? *I* can take care of it; we *won't* have another child, but please don't . . . leave me like that – such . . . silent . . . sad, disgusted . . . love.

TOBIAS (*mumbled, inaudible*) I didn't want you to have to.

AGNES Sir?

TOBIAS (*numb*) I didn't want you to have to . . . you know.

AGNES (*laughs in spite of herself*) Oh, that was thoughtful of
  you! Like a pair of adolescents in a rented room or in the
  family car. Doubtless you hated it as much as I.

TOBIAS (*softly*) Yes.

AGNES But wouldn't let me help you.

TOBIAS (*ibid*) No.

AGNES (*irony*) Which is why you took to your own sweet room
  instead.

TOBIAS (*ibid*) Yes.

AGNES The theory being pat: that a half a loaf is worse than
  none. That you are racked with guilt – stupidly! and *I*
  must *suffer* for it.

(pp. 88–9)

This tragic conversation is a reflection of the way the couple
have always made decisions. Each has always assumed that the
other has been in charge:

TOBIAS (*quiet, rhetorical*) What are we going to do?

AGNES What did you decide?

TOBIAS (*pause, they smile*) Nothing.

AGNES Well you must. Your house is not in order, sir. It's
  full to bursting.

TOBIAS Yes, you've got to help me here.

AGNES No, I don't *think* so.

(p. 84)

This conversation takes place at the height of the crisis. The
way Agnes deals with this is to place the onus of responsibility
onto her husband. She cannot see her own part in this. She
honestly believes that she has been following her husband's lead,
taking her cue from his behaviour rather than asking directly.
Depending on this kind of communication can prove to be very
misleading. What happens is that decisions are masked or even
lost in the confused communication. Agnes's confusion is reflected in the issue of Julia's home-coming. When Julia phones
to say she has left her husband and will be arriving shortly,
Agnes's response is ambivalent:

181

AGNES   Tobias, you will be unhappy to know it, I suppose, or of mixed emotions, certainly, but Julia is coming home.

CLAIRE (*a brief laugh*)   Naturally.

TOBIAS   Yes?

AGNES   She is leaving Douglas, which is no surprise to *me*.

TOBIAS   But, wasn't Julia happy? You didn't tell me anything about. . . .

AGNES   If Julia were happy, she would not be coming home. *I* don't want her here, God knows. I mean she's welcome, of course. . . .

CLAIRE   Right on schedule, once every three years. . . .

AGNES (*closes her eyes for a moment to keep ignoring Claire*) . . . it *is* her home, we are her parents, the *two* of us, and we have our obligations to her, and I have reached an age, Tobias, when I wish we were always alone, you and I, without . . . hangers-on . . . or anyone.

CLAIRE (*cheerful but firm*)   Well, I'm not going.

AGNES   . . . but if she and Doug are through – and I'm not suggesting *she* is in the right – then her place is properly here, as for some it is not.

(pp. 29–30)

Here she is giving a confused message to her husband and sister. She does not really want Julia home but if that is what her daughter wants, then it is her place. Yet later in the play she turns on Tobias and blames him; it is all his fault for not taking a clear stand:

AGNES   . . . and I must live with it, resign myself one marriage more, and wait, and hope that Julia's motherhood will come . . . one day, one marriage.

(p. 88)

Tobias is in a terrible dilemma. Through a number of circumstances he is forced to try and take some kind of stand. The suffering he has to go through is, in part, a result of his life-style; he has never shared the problems of decision-making and thereby avoided responsibility for things that happened in the family. The pressures in the situation become unbearable. Something has to be done, right or wrong. Tobias finds himself totally alone with no help from any quarter. He chooses first to try and do something about his friends:

TOBIAS . . . we love each other, don't we? (*Shout*.) DON'T
WE? DON'T WE LOVE EACH OTHER? (*Soft again, laughter and
tears with it*.) Doesn't friendship grow to that? To love?
Doesn't forty years amount to anything? We've cast our lot
together, boy, we're friends, we've been through lots of
thick or thin together. Which is it, boy? (*Shout*.) WHICH IS
IT, BOY? THICK?! Thin?!. . . . (*Soft*.) Fact I like you well
enough, but not enough . . . that best friend in the world
should be something else . . . more – well, that's my
poverty. So bring your wife and bring your terror, and
bring your plague. (*Loud*.) BRING YOUR PLAGUE! I DON'T
WANT YOU HERE! YOU ASKED?! NO! I DON'T! (*Loud*.) BUT BY
CHRIST, YOU ARE GOING TO STAY HERE! YOU'VE GOT THE
RIGHT. THE RIGHT! DO YOU KNOW THE WORD! THE RIGHT!
(*Soft*.) You've put nearly forty years in it, baby, so have I
and if it's nothing, I don't give a damn, you've got the
right to be here, you've earned it. (*Loud*.) AND BY GOD
YOU'RE GOING TO TAKE IT! DO YOU HEAR ME?! YOU BRING
YOUR TERROR AND YOU COME IN HERE AND YOU LIVE WITH
US. YOU BRING YOUR PLAGUE! YOU STAY WITH US! I DON'T
WANT YOU HERE! I DON'T LOVE YOU! BUT BY GOD. . . . YOU
STAY!
(*Pause*.)
(*Pause*.)

STAY! (*Softer*.) Stay! (*Soft, tears*.) Stay. Please? Stay?
(*Pause*.) Stay? Please stay?
(*A silence in the room. Harry, numb, rises; the women come into
the room slowly, stand. The play is quiet and subdued from now
until the end*.)

(pp. 101–3)

In a desperate move, to remove himself from a self-imposed
double-bind, Tobias takes both sides of the conflict and begs
Harry to choose for him. Harry does and leaves and he and
Tobias go upstairs to pack the bags. And so the decision is made
but once more it is not made by Tobias. This is not surprising if
we, for a moment, lift our heads from the page and view Tobias's
situation. He helps maintain his sister-in-law as an alcoholic; he
accepts his 36-year-old daughter in the role of a spoiled child; he
doesn't have the courage to say no to his friends, he did not have

the strength to allow his wife the child she so desperately wanted. Tobias devoted his life to avoiding conflict and suffering. He just wants to be liked by everyone. The state of decision is clear commitment. It involves risk, the loss of other alternatives and sometimes hurt. It requires of us that we take a stand toward other people; Tobias never has and probably never will be prepared to do this.

The content and style of one's decision-making are an integral part of one's life-style. Once one's life-style achieves a certain level of predictability, we can define this as a 'role'.

Roles

There is much confusion centring on the concept of 'role'. Inasmuch as definitions tend to be individualistic and functional for the purposes of whoever is writing, we shall maintain the tradition. For the purposes of this study, role is defined as 'conforming more or less closely to a pattern of norms and expectations which determine the way in which we behave' (Cotgrove, 1969).

We have a clear (if inaccurate!) image of such people as school teachers, vicars, psychiatrists and nuns. We would be disconcerted if we found a school teacher taking hard drugs or shocked if we discovered nuns at a sexual orgy. The expectations we have of them become almost rules for such people and they are forced to follow them if they do not wish to be discredited. We expect people to behave the same most of the time. If someone we know starts to behave very differently we will probably feel very disturbed and seek some explanation which will take care of our feelings. Our lives are built on routine and predictability. A housewife knows when her husband will be coming home, and he knows what time dinner will be served. When this kind of predictability is disturbed, we are faced with the possible choice of reorganizing our behaviour and accepting the change or fighting to preserve the *status quo*.

When a person in the family has an established role, such as the 'provider', a role which usually falls to the male, a crisis may be precipitated if he is unable to fulfil the obligations which have always been associated with such a position. If the wife in the family suddenly announces that she is going to get a full-time job and thus will no longer do all the household tasks as she has done in the past, she might meet some very strong opposition. In both cases a change in one's personal role affects the whole family. As with the nuns and school teachers cited earlier, there tends to be strong pressure within the family for members to remain the same. The Albee family displayed a constellation of roles. Each member has at least two roles. Tobias is the peace-lover and hotel keeper. Agnes is the maintenance woman and the martyr, Claire the clown and the scapegoat. Julia shares with her this latter role but also plays the spoiled child. Tobias does not like unpleasantness. What he wants is a peaceful life. Agnes sums up their life together:

> AGNES . . . There are no mountains in my life . . . nor chasms. It is a rolling, pleasant land . . . verdant, my darling, thank you.
>
> TOBIAS (*cutting a cigar*) We do what we can.
>
> AGNES (*little laugh*) Our motto. If we should ever go downhill, have a crest made, join things, we must have that put in Latin — We do what we can, on your blazers, over the mantel: maybe we could do it on the linen as, well . . .
>
> (pp. 16–17)

Whenever anything discomforting is about to happen, Tobias immediately attempts to smooth things over by acting as the genial host or the peace-maker. Claire is a source of conflict between Tobias and Agnes. Tobias doesn't want to acknowledge this. Agnes is very clear that Claire is an alcoholic. Tobias not only simply refuses to acknowledge this reality but actively helps Claire to remain alcoholic by feeding her drinks all the time. At the beginning of the play whilst Tobias and Agnes are talking, Claire enters the room:

> TOBIAS (*sees Claire standing uncomfortably away from them*) Ah, there you are. I said to Agnes just a moment ago. . .
>
> CLAIRE (*to Agnes' back, a rehearsed speech, gone through but hated*) I must apologize, Agnes. I'm . . . very sorry.
>
> AGNES (*not looking at her, mock surprise*) But what are you sorry *for*, Claire?

CLAIRE   I apologize that my nature is such to bring out in
you the full force of your brutality.

TOBIAS (*to placate*)   Look, now, I think we can do without
any of this sort of. . . .

(pp. 18–19)

This is Tobias's way of moving into his role of keeping things
nice and calm. This time he fails and Agnes speaks her mind:

AGNES (*rises from her chair, proceeds toward exit*) *If* you come
to the dinner table unsteady, *if* when you try to say good
evening and weren't the autumn colours lovely today you
are nothing but vowels and *if* one smells the vodka on you
from across the room – and *don't* tell me again, *either* of
you! that vodka leaves nothing on the breath; if you are
expecting, if you are sadly and wearily expecting it, it
does, – *if* these conditions exist . . . *persist* . . . then the
reaction of one who is burdened by her love is not
brutality – though it would be excused, believe me! – not
brutality at all, but the souring side of love. If I scold, it
is because I wish I needn't. If I am sharp, it is because I
am neither less nor more than human. . . . Well, be kind
to Claire, dear. She is . . . injured.
(*Exits. A brief silence.*)

TOBIAS   Ah, well.

CLAIRE   I have never known whether to applaud or cry. Or,
rather, I never know which would be the more appreciated –
expected.

TOBIAS (*rather sadly*)   You are a great damn fool.

CLAIRE (*sadly*)   Yes. Why is she calling Julia?

TOBIAS   Do you want a quick brandy before she comes back?

(pp. 19–20)

Unable this time to prevent the quarrel from becoming public,
Tobias manages to salvage something by offering Claire a drink
and thereby telling Claire at least that they are still friends. When
Agnes returns to find Claire drinking, a pitched battle com-
mences. Tobias is completely inadequate, and after a few feeble
attempts to cool things down, he simply gives up:

AGNES (*walking by Claire*)   My, what an odd glass to put a soft
drink in. Tobias, you have a quiet sense of humour after all.

TOBIAS Now Agnes. . . .

CLAIRE He has no. . . .

AGNES (*quiet, tight smile, ignoring Claire*) It *would* serve you right my dear Tobias were I to go away, drift off. You would not have a woman left about you – only Claire and Julia, not even people. . . . it would serve you right.

CLAIRE (*great mocking*) But I'm not an alcoholic, baby!

TOBIAS She . . . she can drink . . . a little.

AGNES (*there is a true passion here: we see under the calm a little*) I WILL NOT TOLERATE IT! ! I WILL NOT HAVE YOU! (*Softer but tight lipped.*) Oh God! I wouldn't mind for a moment if you filled your bath tub with it, lowered yourself in it, DROWNED! I rather wish you would. . . .

TOBIAS Please, Agnes. . . .

AGNES What I cannot stand is the selfishness! Those of you who want to die . . . and take your whole lives doing it.

CLAIRE (*lazy, but with loathing under it*) Your wife is a perfectionist; they are VERY difficult to live with, these people.

TOBIAS (*to Agnes, a little pleading in it*) She isn't an alcoholic. . . . she says; she can drink some.

AGNES We think that's very nice. We shall all rest easier to know it is wilful: that the vomit and the tears, the muddy mind, the falls and the absences, the cigarettes out on the table tops, the calls from the club to come and get you please . . . that they are all . . . wilful, that it *can* be helped. (*Scathing, but softly.*) If you are not an alcoholic, you are beyond forgiveness.

CLAIRE (*ibid*) Well, I've been that for a long time haven't I, sweetheart?

(pp. 28–9)

Tobias's apparent impotence has special meaning here. The argument between Claire and Agnes is bringing out into the open the conflicts that threaten the delicate balance of this tangle. Tobias must almost become a juggler; he cannot afford to offend or alienate either of the two women, for he needs them both.

Tobias is capable of growing angry. He does so with his own daughter but even then cannot escape being caught up in his own feelings:

187

TOBIAS This isn't the first time, you know. This isn't the first time you've come back with one of your goddamned marriages on the rocks. Four! Count 'em!

JULIA (*rage*) I know how many marriages I've gotten myself into, you. . . .

TOBIAS Four! You expect to come back here, nestle in to being fifteen and misunderstood each time!? You are thirty-six years old, for God's sake! . . .

JULIA And you are one hundred! Easily!

TOBIAS Thirty-six! Each time! Dragging your . . . your – I was going to say pride – your marriage with you like some Raggedy Anne doll, by the foot. You, you fill this house with your whining. . . .

JULIA I DON'T ASK TO COME BACK HERE.

TOBIAS YOU BELONG HERE.

(*Heavy breathing from both of them, finally a little rueful giggle. Tobias speaks rather nonchalantly now.*)

TOBIAS Well. Now that I've taken out on my only daughter the disgust of my declining years, I'll mix a very good and very strong martini. Join me?

(pp. 47–8)

This is an honest confrontation by Tobias. His daughter is all that he says she is, but having said it, he immediately disqualifies it. The final message that the daughter must get is that her behaviour really doesn't matter to him. In this way, he enjoys the relationship the way it is. One of the things it allows is for him to continue to be the patient and understanding peace-maker. The qualities that Tobias displays as a peace-maker would be fine if he were a member of the Diplomatic Corps but they are inadequate in the role of husband and father. His refusal to deal with conflict serves only to contribute to the eventual crisis. A family that has never learned how to cope with its own internal conflicts lessens its chances of survival and becomes subjected to external pressures. Thus it is they are so easily precipitated into a crisis by the arrival of Harry and Edna. For the 'plague' they are accused of bringing with them exists already within the Albee family.

The roles of Agnes and Tobias are complementary because of the way each behaves. This has the effect of each locking the other into their respective roles. While Tobias is playing peace-maker,

Agnes is maintaining. Whilst Tobias is playing host, Agnes is suffering. The interesting thing is that Agnes is aware of this but does nothing.

> AGNES 'To keep in shape', have you heard the expression?
> Most people misunderstand it, assume it means alteration,
> when it does not. Maintenance. When we keep something
> in shape, we maintain its shape – whether we are proud of
> that shape or not, is another matter – we keep *it* from
> falling apart. We do not attempt the impossible. We
> maintain, we hold.
> JULIA Yes? So?
> AGNES (*quietly*) I shall . . . keep this family in shape. I shall
> maintain it. Hold it.
>
> (pp. 57–8)

In our society the traditional role of the woman is that of the housewife. It doesn't take much imagination to see how this role can very easily evolve into the role that Agnes has. The problem of the therapist is to help the woman move out of this role into a new one and in this way help her to fulfil her needs as a person in a more healthy way. We have discussed the scapegoat syndrome in some depth in the Royal Family. Here we would merely like to demonstrate briefly how the two scapegoat roles function in the Albee family. Claire and Julia take the role of scapegoats, Claire as the alcoholic, Julia as the spoiled child. These roles are very useful to Agnes and Tobias. While they exist, there will always be a reason for their unhappiness. They can continue to subscribe to the perfect relationship myth. Claire, in addition to being the alcoholic, is the clown of the family. This is a very important role because through her humour the family is helped to avoid the pain. She takes it upon herself. If we think of Claire in relation to Tobias and Agnes, we can almost think in terms of a contract. Each of the *ménage à trois* gains something special from the arrangement. First of all Claire is allowed to be an alcoholic, receiving support and friendship from Tobias. This allows Tobias to take the role of protector and benefactor, while receiving sympathy from her as being the misunderstood husband. Agnes can continue to stand alone playing the role of the martyr, whilst blaming Claire for her unhappiness. And we have the image of Claire the drunk, the clown, with a perceptive eye; the angry clown with the bitter tongue. In her role as a clown, Claire can rescue the family from itself. At one point, Agnes, Tobias and Julia begin to argue over Harry and Edna, sleeping in Julia's old room. As in a circus ring, the tension slowly begins to mount. Agnes turns on Julia:

> AGNES (*swinging around to face her quite hard*) Well, why don't you run upstairs and claim your goddam room back! Barricade yourself in there! Push a bureau in front of the door! Take Tobias' pistol while you're at it! Arm yourself!
> (*A burst from an accordion; Claire appears in the archway wearing it.*)
> CLAIRE Barricades? Pistols? Really? So soon?
> JULIA (*giggling in spite of herself*) Oh, Claire. . . .
> AGNES (*not amused*) Claire, will you take off that damned thing!
> CLAIRE They laughed when I sat down to the accordion. Take if off? No, I will not! This is going to be a festive night, from the smell of it, and sister Claire wants to do her part – pay her way, so to speak . . . justify.
> AGNES You're not going to play that dreadful instrument in here, and. . . .
> (*But the rest of what she wants to say is drowned out by the chords from the accordion.*)
> Tobias? (*Calm.*) Do something about that.
> TOBIAS (*he too, chuckling*) Oh, now Agnes.
> CLAIRE So. (*Another chord.*) Shall I wait? Shall I start now? A polka? What?
>
> (pp. 59–60)

So we see at just the right moment the clown jumped through the hoop. The timing could not be better. The confrontation between mother and daughter is diverted, masked. One can almost sense the relief that Claire's entry brings with it. But Claire can also use humour to tell the family some home-truths:

> CLAIRE . . . and here comes Julia, home from the wars, four purple hearts. . . .
> JULIA Why don't you just have another drink and stop it, Claire?
> CLAIRE (*looks at her empty glass, shrugs*) All right.
> JULIA (*rather defensive*) I have *left* Doug. We are not *divorced*.

CLAIRE Yet! Are you cooking a second batch, Tobias?
(*Back to Julia.*) But you've come back home, haven't you?
And didn't you – with the others?
JULIA (*her back up*) Where else am I supposed to go?
CLAIRE It's a great big world, baby. There are hotels, new
cities. Home is the quickest road to Reno, I know of.
JULIA (*condescending*) You've had a lot of experience in these
matters, Claire.
CLAIRE Side-lines! Good seats, right on the fifty yard line,
objective observer. (*Texas accent or near it.*) I swar! Ef ah
did'nt luv mah sister so, ah'd say she'd got yuh hitched
fur the pleasure uh getting yuh back.
JULIA ALL RIGHT.
TOBIAS THAT WILL DO NOW!
CLAIRE (*in the silence that follows*) Sorry. Very . . . very sorry.

(p. 53)

The alcoholic has a very special role in the family. There tends
to be a pattern of repeated behaviour surrounding the alcoholic.
Writing on different kinds of alcoholics Max Glatt, in a book called
The Alcoholic and the Help he Needs (1970), quotes Thelma
Whalen and writes about a typology of different personality types
in wives of alcoholics. Whalen calls them 'Suffering Susan',
whose need to be miserable is gratified by her marriage to an
alcoholic; 'Controlling Catherine' who marries a man whom she
regards as somewhat inadequate or inferior to her; 'Wavering
Winifred', who herself is fearful and insecure, and feels secure
in a relationship with a man only as long as she feels he cannot
get along without her and needs her – her tolerance wears thin
when her husband's drinking gets too far out of control; and
finally 'Punitive Polly', whose relationship to her husband resembles that of a boa constrictor to a rabbit – the rabbit sometimes
likes being swallowed, though at other times may rebel and go
out and get drunk.

In all such marriages the alcoholic's behaviour is only one
factor in the family situation which produces emotional problems.
Certainly such (and other) types of wives of alcoholics are seen
quite often, but frequently they may all be temporary phases during
a wife's desperate and long-drawn-out effort to detect – by a
method of trial and error – how she can transform her husband

(who has changed so completely since he started to drink to excess) back to the man he was at the time she married him.

Also within the family there can be a variety of responses. Agnes sees Claire as the reprobate, beyond help. Tobias responds by denial of any problems. In this way the needs of both are satisfied and there is no need for Claire to change her behaviour. Finally there is Julia the spoiled child. Once more she runs home after her fourth marriage breakdown.

How do Tobias and Agnes handle their daughter's return? Agnes makes the clear statement that she wants to be alone with Tobias, with no other people around. With this feeling one would expect her to be firm, even harsh with Julia – certainly the last that one would expect would be strong material sympathy:

> CLAIRE (*peers into her glass, over-curious*)   I have been trying, without very much success, to find out why Miss Julie here is come home.
>
> AGNES   I would imagine that Julia is home because she wishes to be, and that is where she belongs if she wants.
>
> (pp. 54–5)

At this point Julia begins to explain something of why her marriage has failed. Again, Agnes handles it in a very odd way for a mother who has stated that what she really wants is for her daughter not to be around so that she can enjoy being alone with her husband.

> AGNES   You needn't make a circus of it: Tell me later when. . . .
>
> (p. 55)

Julia persists, and Agnes insists, even to the point of providing her daughter with excuses not to speak about her marriage:

> AGNES (*to Julia*)   You're tired: We'll talk about it after. . . .
>
> (p. 55)

Later in the play we learn what Agnes means when she says 'We'll talk about it later'.

> AGNES (*to Tobias*)   . . . . the soothing recapitulation. You don't go through it, my love: the history. Nothing is calmed by a pat on the back, a gentle massage, or slowly,

slowly combing the hair, no: the history, Teddy's birth,
and how she felt unwanted, tricked; his death, and was
she more relieved than lost. . . . All the schools that we
sent her to, and did she fail them through hate . . . or love?
And when we came to marriage dear: each one of them,
the fear, the happiness, the sex, the stopping, the
infidelities. . . . .

(p. 72)

What game is Agnes playing here? There are two very confused
messages that she is sending out: though she doesn't want Julia
home – and yet says it is her place; though she doesn't enjoy the
task of 'comforting' her daughter – yet we have already seen
that she schemes in order to insure that such a situation is set up.
Tobias, too, gives out confused messages to Julia:

TOBIAS . . . You expect to come back here, nestle into being
    fifteen and misunderstood each time! You are thirty-six
    years old, for God's sake! . . .
JULIA And you are one hundred! Easily!
TOBIAS Thirty-six! Each time! Dragging your . . . your – I
    was going to say pride – your marriage with you like some
    Raggedy Anne doll, by the foot. You, fill this house with
    your whining. . . .
JULIA (rage) I DON'T ASK TO COME BACK HERE!
TOBIAS YOU BELONG HERE!
(Heavy breathing from both of them, finally a little rueful giggle.
Tobias speaks rather nonchantly now.)
    Well. Now that I have taken out on my only daughter
    the . . . disgust of my declining years, I'll mix a very good
    and very strong martini. Join me?

(p. 48)

What meaning can we get out of this encounter? Tobias's first
statement seems a reasonably accurate description of Julia's
behaviour. And yet, by the end, he has retracted what he has said,
and in fact seems to be saying that her behaviour is fine. 'Join me
for a drink? It seems very obvious, that, despite statements to the
opposite effect, both parents are quite prepared to allow their
daughter's childish behaviour to continue. Particularly this
becomes apparent after the episode in which Julia enters the room

with a gun in an attempt to get rid of Edna and Harry. At first
Agnes displays real anger ('You should be horse whipped, young
lady'), but inevitably and quickly reverses her attitude – 'Ah – ah;
let me comb your hair, and rub your back . . . and we shall soothe
. . . and solve . . . and fall to sleep.'

Looking at the situation as it exists for Julia it is obvious that
she, too, derives certain benefits from her role. Like the child,
whenever anything goes wrong she can run home to mummy and
daddy; there she will receive comfort, the pressure will be taken
off her, and she no longer has to face the difficulties that having
adult relationships with men bring. Home is safe and secure,
predictable and non-threatening. How unstable she is in a strange
situation is clearly seen by the way she reacts upon her return
home. At first, a purely selfish reaction:

> JULIA   Yes! What *about* that! I come home: my room is full
> of Harry and Edna. I have no place to put my things. . . .
> What are they *doing* here? Don't they have a house any more?
>
> (p. 43)

Julia sees herself as displaced by the guests despite the fact
that she must have known them all her life. Her room is taken
over, the family is disrupted, her parents upset. She responds as
any small child might: she becomes possessive and hysterical.
Edna and Harry are sleeping in her room:

> AGNES (*patient*)   Go up to my room and lie down.
> JULIA (*an ugly laugh*)   Your room!
> EDNA (*calm*)   You may go and lie down in our room if you
> like.
> JULIA (*a trapped woman surrounded*)   Your room! (*To
> Agnes.*) Your room? MINE! ! (*Looks from one to the other,
> sees only waiting faces.*) MINE! !
> HARRY (*makes a move toward the side-board*)   God!
> JULIA   Don't go near that!
> AGNES   Julia. . . .
> JULIA   I want!
> CLAIRE (*sad smile*)   What do you want Julia?
> JULIA   I. . . .
> HARRY   Jesus!
> JULIA   I WANT . . . WHAT IS MINE! . . .
>
> (p. 67)

Thus the relationship between Julia and her parents seems to be a symbiotic one: Julia's problems are solved by being able to run away from her personal conflicts to a warm, accepting environment that will accept her immaturity; and Agnes and Tobias are given what they will perceive as a real problem to cope with – a problem that will prevent the need for them to look at their own relationship.

The Albee family is not that unusual. This is the kind of family we often see in treatment. We have seen how all the roles complement each other within a dynamic if unstable family. It should also be clear that a change in any one role will inevitably lead to changes in all the others. It is a question of who will make the first move. Change is thus a risk. Because the consequences are not completely predictable. If for a moment we try to imagine Agnes, what would happen if she changed in such a way that she insisted on reversing her role and became the decision-maker. The first thing she would do is place strong limits on Claire's drinking or get rid of her completely. Either way would probably lead to a complete rejection unless Claire made some pretty big changes. Agnes would demand clear response from Tobias, he would no longer be allowed to vacillate and opt out of conflicts. There would be no more comforting for Julia, she would have to act her age, and behave like a 36-year-old woman.

The other alternative is that the family would strive hard to prevent Agnes from changing. If this ploy was unsuccessful, she might well be rejected.

Any significant role change brings with it the possibility that certain relationships will not be able to survive the change.

Survival

Change is possible, but difficult. This is true in all life, whether it is the society as a whole, or the individual. Present day America is involved in great conflict between Black and White people. Periodically the conflict erupts into open violence. Meanwhile some people quietly demonstrate that integration is a realistic possibility – even to the point of marrying.

Because change is so difficult, many people are prepared to

invest all their energies in maintaining the *status quo* rather than seeking new solutions. There is an uncertainty factor in change – in a sense it is a risk. If we see the risk as being too great, then we may prefer to stay as we are. It is around this balance point that disturbed or destructive behaviour may emerge. Gherke and Kirschenbaum, in a paper on family survival (1967, pp. 78–9) say 'A family becomes sick when members perceive efforts towards growth as a threat towards the survival of their family unit'.

An example which may illustrate this point comes from the personal knowledge of the authors:

> This is a story of a family in crisis. The father died of cancer and shortly afterwards the eldest daughter married. This left the mother and her 14-year-old son together. Mother went into severe depression, rarely leaving the house, and having contact with few people. After a while the social worker became involved because the son was consistently away from school. He was then labelled school phobic and sent to an adolescent treatment centre in the neighbouring town. There he blossomed, appearing cheerful and bright. He was returned home after three months apparently cured. Then the pattern was repeated. In discussion with the child shortly after this point, it was discovered that he was afraid that his mother would die if she was left alone. As far as we know things have remained pretty much the same – the *status quo* is being preserved.

The example also highlights the central concept in family therapy – that to isolate an individual in such a case is almost useless, for the problem lies within the relationship between the family members, and not in the individual himself. Further, we can draw another important lesson that many therapists will have learned: that it is possible for the individual to invest his whole existence in the family. It occasionally happens, for instance in automobile accidents or war, that all but one of the family are killed. The survivor immediately becomes the target for a special kind of sympathy. Either social work agencies or relatives attempt very quickly to become substitute families. People feel very sorry for a person who loses his family in such a way, and find it difficult to imagine that he can survive without one.

Few people want to be alone, because then there is only self.

This is dramatized on special occasions, such as Christmas. The fear that one may not survive being alone is a part of this experience. Other people recognize this, and will often attempt to help one avoid the experience, and such an individual may find himself besieged with invitations.

The 'Survival Myth' is compounded of this fear that we may be rejected, if we act too differently. Each person carries within himself the image, which one may almost liken to a set of blueprints, of what a family should be like. This is learned from a person's experiences in his own family. The internalizing of this image is an on-going process throughout life. Some people experience difficulties because of this image when they begin their own families, because the reality is always different from the image. This discrepancy may provoke great anxiety and evoke the fear that the family may not survive. Laing describes this fear (1970, pp. 13, 15):

> Persons do manifestly try to set on the 'inner' worlds of others to preserve their own inner worlds, and others (so-called obsessionals, for instance) arrange and re-arrange the external world of objects to preserve their inner worlds. There is no systematic psychoanalytic theory of the nature of transpersonal defences, whereby self attempts to regulate the inner life of the other in order to preserve his own, nor of techniques of coping with such persecution by others. . . .
>
> In some families parents cannot allow children to break the 'family' down within themselves, if that is what they want to do, because this is felt as the break-up of the family, and then where will it end? For the child also the 'family' may be an internal structure more important than the 'breast', 'penis', 'mother', or 'father'. As long as the family is felt as permanent much also can be impermanent.
>
> The 'family' becomes a medium to link its members, whose links with one another may otherwise be very attenuated. A crisis will occur if any member of the family wishes to leave by getting the 'family' out of his system, or dissolving the 'family' in himself. Within the family, the 'family' may be felt as the whole world. To destroy the 'family' may be experienced as worse than murder or more selfish than suicide. 'It would be to destroy my parents'

world' and felt as much by the parents. And what the
parents do may be felt by the children as shattering if it
breaks up the 'family' as well as the family. Dilemmas abound.
If I do not destroy the 'family' the 'family' will destroy me.
I cannot destroy the 'family' in myself without destroying
'it' in them. Feeling themselves endangered, will they destroy
me? Acts not so motivated or intended are defined by the
others as destructive, or persecutory, or sick because they
entail the break-up of their 'family'. Each must sacrifice
himself therefore to preserve the 'family'. The 'family' comes
to serve as a defence or bulwark against total collapse,
disintegration, emptiness, despair, guilt, and other terrors.
The preservation, change, or dissolution of the 'family' is not
allowed to be a purely private affair when the 'family' has to
be felt to be preserved by all its members. Loss of a family
member may be less dangerous than a new addition to the
family if the new recruit imports another 'family' into the
'family'. Hence the preservation of the 'family' is equated
with the preservation of self and world and the dissolution
of the 'family' inside another is equated with death of self
and world collapse. Alternatively one hates or fears the
'family', or envies others their happiness or contented family
life; the world will collapse if the 'family' is not assassinated.

In the paper entitled 'Survival Patterns in Family Conjoint
Therapy' (1967), Gherke and Kirschenbaum identify three major
survival patterns in disturbed families. They define the survival
myth in a way very similar to Laing (p. 68):

It became apparent that the disturbed family's interaction
and communication pattern, covert rules, and symptomology
may define the pattern of survival on which the family
operates. The family system is geared toward the defence of
the illusions shared by each family member about the role
each must play in order to support the parental relationship
and thus maintain the family balance.

The first pattern we may call 'delinquent'. For example, we
may call the Royal Family a delinquent family because the only
way the family can be preserved is for Hamlet to become a scapegoat. The Royal Family is unusual in that the threat to the family

is real, in that Claudius has actually committed murder. For most families the threat exists in fantasy form – for example, in the Loman family we have had such a situation. Biff is delinquent in that he follows values antithetical to the family – he steals and goes to jail. And then, when we examine the relationship between Linda and Willy, we find Linda full of fear in regard to what might happen to Willy if she is honest.

The second pattern is 'suicidal'. As Gherke and Kirschenbaum say (1967, p. 73):

> The survival myth in these families is that no one can function alone, and that no member is whole without the others, and that, therefore, the family cannot survive if any member leaves it. They are all caught, and extremely frightened.

A case history at this point might illustrate this pattern:

> The family consisted of grandmother, mother, stepfather, and 18-year-old son. The sexual relationship between mother and stepfather was poor. The mother continued to attempt to seduce her son whilst denying that this was what she was doing. The son was unable to perceive leaving the family as a realistic alternative – which obviously, at age 18, it was. The only way he could handle his disturbed feelings was to take hard drugs. One night whilst high on drugs with a friend, and listening to rock music, the boys became involved in playing Russian roulette. The son died. He finally managed to escape.

The third pattern involves the Albee family. This is called 'repressive'. This family will be marked by the fear of open aggression. To quote Gherke and Kirschenbaum again (1967, p. 68):

> The substance of the myth is that impulsive expressions of feelings are precipitent actions, and will bring about loss of love, even abandonment, especially when these feelings or actions are released in the face of opposing feelings or actions of other members of the family.

Each member of the Albee family has their own way of protecting themselves in terms of surviving within the family system.

199

All of the people are marked by varying degrees of loneliness and alienation – it is as if each person has their own niche. But at the same time they need the others.

Tobias, as we have already seen, is the one who avoids feelings the most. Claire knows when to stop clowning and back down. Agnes sees herself as the one who keeps the family in balance, and this includes controlling all unpleasantness so that it does not become too disruptive. Julia is the only one who is allowed to break the pattern, but it is all right for her as she is the child, and acts out for everyone else.

The family which is caught up in the survival myth contains a great deal of fantasy and fear. The therapist is faced with a number of challenges. The first task is to analyse and understand the particular communication pattern in the family as it relates to the survival myth. At this point the role of the therapist becomes that of a teacher; he must demonstrate the falsity of the myth by having the family take risks in the areas in which they show fear. This is like asking them 'What is the worst that can happen if you do that?' Very occasionally it is true that the fears will be realized – for example the father may leave the family or a member may become violent. What is important here is that the individuals now have the chance to deal with real situations. Of equal, if not greater importance, is that the removal of the fantasy and fear is the first step towards allowing free growth and development.

We conclude this section by quoting from the article 'Survival Patterns in Family Conjoint Therapy' (Gherke and Kirschenbaum, 1967, p. 79), where it is a reality that we need other people to survive:

> We think the Reality Survival Concept is based on the premise that each person in the marital relationship must operate as a whole person. By this we mean each may be dependent on the other in many ways but not for survival. Each is responsible for his own growth. His survival must be dependent on his ability to achieve that growth through open and direct expression of his desires and limitations. The marital partners must be able to accept such expression from each other as an indication of their differentness. This involves perceiving differentness at its best as potentially enhancing to the relationship, and at its worst as somewhat

limiting; if it is seen as an attack or intent to undermine, the relationship cannot grow. A 'working' marital relationship in reality, then, is not a blending or meshing of two individuals into a whole person. It is the accomplishment of two individuals to remain intact in their individuality so that their individual growth falls concurrently. Ideally, the growth of each is then enhanced by the growth of the other although it may be in different directions or at different rates of progress. This is accomplished because of the process utilized by each to express himself and perceive the other's individuality without threat.

Conclusion

Family therapy is still in a state of flux. There is no consensus of methodology. A few years ago an attempt was made to organize family therapists in America into a professional association. The attempt failed. The chief rationale given for this was that the whole field was still evolving, and that it was too early to attempt to formulate its specific schools of thought under one aegis in family therapy.

We have offered one model for analysing the family. We have almost exclusively been concerned with the communication between family members and how this relates to the behaviour of the members. Other therapists will make different approaches. For example, some base their treatment on psychoanalysis, others on behavioural theory. But the field is rich in its diversity – yet other techniques for family therapy include pastoral counselling, non-directive therapy, encounter groups and Gestalt therapy. Not only does the underlying theory differ, but the structuring of the therapeutic milieu differs from therapist to therapist. Some will only ever see the whole family together, others prefer to view the family serially and individually. The combinations are endless.

The field of family therapy is like an enormous supermarket – one can enter and shop around looking for a product to meet one's needs. One of the field's basic strengths is its diversity – it is continually producing new insights, new techniques, new ideas. Yet its strength is also part of its weakness. Enormously creative yet enormously disorganized, family therapy lacks systematization and exhaustive analysis. The research that has been done is mainly descriptive, and thus cannot hope to meet any rigorous scientific appraisal. Part of the reason can be found in the ethical problem, and part in the very complexity of the subject. For example, one area which cries out for study is the role of the therapist, and of how much his personality influences the family. This is an important question in family therapy, for whatever his school of thought, he cannot help but be a model and teacher for the family.

However, the value of family therapy cannot be dismissed. It is here to stay, despite its present limitations, its many internal differences, and the basic lack of research. When we realize that there are such families in the community as the ones we have described in this book, then the value of such a treatment mode becomes obvious. Families today are in trouble.

Laing, in *The Politics of Experience*, presented the remarkable truth that a child born today stands more chance of going to a mental hospital than of going to university. One woman in six will receive some kind of psychiatric treatment in hospital. The current divorce rate indicates that more than 100,000 people will be divorced this year in England. This last figure indicates that a new attitude is growing towards marriage. The once sacred institution is becoming more casual. 'The family' does indeed seem to be in trouble. The once basic socializing unit is no longer adequate to the demands placed on it. Today the school is coming under critical appraisal as an institution to take over more and more of the responsibilities of the family.

If the family is going to survive it will have to undergo some severe reappraisal. When two people wish to be married, about the only demand likely to be placed on them is a medical check to see if they have venereal disease. We behave as if every individual is completely capable of creating a good marriage and a healthy family. We can imagine how long an engineering firm would stay in business if it assumed that every single person automatically had the skills of an engineer. We can almost say today that the family is bankrupt. Perhaps it is about time that we began to think of training people who express desire to become husbands or wives or parents – training in such skills as communication, decision-making, developmental psychology, etc. We can no longer avoid facing such issues. And perhaps, rather than wait until a few months before marriage, we can start much earlier – in the primary school.

We are, of course, talking of imposing our values on people, perhaps even by law. These values include clear communication, honesty, trust, valuing, responsibility, etc. If by starting in the primary schools we are accused of trying to brain-wash, then we agree. We accept our responsibility.

Note

1 Dr Joel Fort, noted expert on drug addiction and alcoholism, in a recent article on 'The Drug Explosion' notes that 'today 35,000,000 Americans use sedatives, stimulants or tranquilizers, mostly obtained legally through their doctors. Despite this medical supervision between 500,000 and 1,000,000 of these have become abusers.' (See *Playboy*, September 1972.)

SUGGESTIONS FOR

FURTHER READING

ACKERMAN, N. W., *Family Psychotherapy in Transition*, Little, Brown, Boston, Mass., 1970, *Treating the Troubled Family*, Basic Books, New York, 1966, *Exploring the Base for Family Therapy* (ed.), Family Service Association of America, New York, 1961. This writer gives a good overview of family therapy. Some illuminating interviews with families give the reader a chance to examine a first class therapist at work.

GOFFMAN, E., *The Presentation of Self in Everyday Life*, Penguin, Harmondsworth, 1971. An excellent analysis of the various roles that people play. How people present themselves in different work situations.

HALEY, J. (ed.), *Changing Families*, Grune & Stratton, New York, 1970. An excellent bedside anthology presenting a number of important family therapy models. Every family therapist should have one.

JACKSON, D. D. (ed.), *The Etiology of Schizophrenia*, Basic Books, New York, 1960. An old book, but still valuable. Presents us with well written articles in a highly complex field.

LAING, R. D., *The Self and Others*, Tavistock Publications, London, 1969. A further look into the area of sanity and madness. Laing continues to challenge modern psychiatry and the book is studded with ideas on every page.

MACGREGOR, R., RITCHIE, A. M., SERRANO, A. C., SCHUSTER, F. P., MCDONALD, E. C. and GOOLISHAN, H. A., *Multiple Impact Therapy with Families*, McGraw Hill, New York, 1964. A detailed description of a family therapy team working with families two days at a time. Well documented and worthwhile reading for therapists who like to work in an unusual way.

PERLS, F. S., *Gestalt Therapy Verbatim*, Bantam Books, London, 1972. A detailed description of how Perls used himself as an active therapist. A must for every therapist.

WATZLAWICK, P., *An Anthology of Human Communication*, Science and Behaviour Books, Palo Alto, Calif., 1965. A good introduction to different forms of communication patterns. It pays particular attention to paradoxical communication. The author also has a fine analysis of Edward Albee's *Who's Afraid of Virginia Woolf?*

SELECT BIBLIOGRAPHY

The Plays

ALBEE, EDWARD: *A Delicate Balance*, Penguin, Harmondsworth, 1969.

BOLT, ROBERT: *A Man For All Seasons*, Heinemann, London, 1967.

ELIOT, T. S.: *The Cocktail Party*, Faber & Faber, 1968.

ELIOT, T. S.: *The Family Reunion*, Faber & Faber, 1968.

IBSEN, HENRIK: *The Wild Duck*, Everyman's Library, Dent, 1958.

MILLER, ARTHUR: *Death of a Salesman*, Penguin, Harmondsworth, 1971.

O'NEILL, EUGENE: *A Long Day's Journey into Night*, Jonathan Cape, London, 1972.

RATTIGAN, TERENCE: *The Winslow Boy*, Pan Books, London, 1971.

SHAKESPEARE, WILLIAM: *Hamlet*, Cambridge University Press, 1971.

SYNGE, J. M.: *Riders to the Sea, Plays, Poems and Prose*, Everyman's Library, Dent, London, 1968.

WILLIAMS, TENNESSEE: *The Glass Menagerie, Sweet Bird of Youth and Other Plays*, Penguin, Harmondsworth, 1971.

The Books

AUBERT, VILHELM: *The Hidden Society*, Free Press, Chicago, Collier-Macmillan, London, 1963.

BATESON, G., JACKSON, D., HALEY, J. and WEAKLAND, D.: 'Towards a Theory of Schizophrenia', *Behavioural Science*, vol. 1, pp. 251–64, 1956.

BECKER, HOWARD S.: *Outsiders*, Collier-Macmillan, New York, 1963.

CAUDILL, W., REDLICH, F. C., GILMORE, H. R. and BRODY, E. B.: 'Social Structure and Interaction Processes on a Psychiatric Ward', *American Journal of Osteopsychiatry*, vol. 22, 324–34, 1952.

COOPER, DAVID: *The Death of the Family*, Penguin, Harmondsworth, 1972.

COTGROVE, STEPHEN: *The Science of Society*, Allen & Unwin, London, 1969.

DAVIS, DEREK RUSSELL: 'A Re-appraisal of Ibsen's *Ghosts*', *Family Process*, 1970.

DEAKIN, MICHAEL: *The Children on the Hill*, André Deutsch, London, 1972.

DUFF, RAYMOND and HOLLINGSHEAD, AUGUST: *Sickness and Society*, Harper & Row, New York, 1968.

DURRELL, LAWRENCE: *The Alexandria Quartet*, Faber & Faber, London, 1970.

ERIKSON, ERIK: *Identity, Youth and Crisis*, Faber & Faber, London, 1968.

FORT, JOEL: 'The Drug Explosion', *Playboy Magazine*, September, 1972.

GHERKE, SHIRLEY and KIRSCHENBAUM, MARTIN: 'Survival Patterns in Family Conjoint Therapy', *Family Process*, vol. 6, no. 1, March 1967.

GINOTT, HAIM: *Between Parent and Child*, Pan Books, London, 1970.

GLATT, MAX: *The Alcoholic and the Help he Needs*, Priory Press, London, 1970.

GOFFMAN, ERVING: *Asylums*, Penguin, Harmondsworth, 1970.

GOLDTHORPE, J. H., LOCKWOOD, D., BECHHOFER, E. and PLATT, JENNIFER: *The Affluent Worker in the Class Structure*, Cambridge University Press, 1971.

GREEN, HANNAH: *I Never Promised you a Rose Garden*, Pan Books, London, 1964.

HELLER, JOSEPH: *Catch-22*, Jonathan Cape, London, 1961.

HUNT, NIGEL: *The World of Nigel Hunt*, Darwen Finlayson, Beaconsfield, 1967.

JAY, ANTHONY: *Corporation Man*, Jonathan Cape, London, 1972.

JONES, ERNEST: *Life and Works of Sigmund Freud*, vol. III: *Last Phase 1919–1939*, Basic Books, New York, 1957, p. 103.

JUNG., C. G.: *Development of the Personality*, Routledge & Kegan Paul, London, 1954.

KANTNOR, ROBERT and HOFFMAN, LYNN: article in *Family Process*, vol. 5, no. 1, March 1966.

KARLEN, ARNO: *Sexuality and Homosexuality*, MacDonald, London, 1971.

KELLER, HELEN: *The Story of My Life*, Hodder & Stoughton, London, 1947.

KOHL, HERBERT, *Thirty-Six Children*, Penguin, Harmondsworth, 1972.

KUBLER-ROSS, ELISABETH: *On Death and Dying*, Tavistock Publications, London, 1970.

LACHMAN, SHELDON J.: *Psychosomatic Disorders: A Behaviouristic Approach*, John Wiley, New York, 1972.

LAING, R. D.: *The Politics of the Family and Other Essays*, Tavistock Publications, London, 1971.

LAING, R. D. and ESTERSON, A.: *Sanity, Madness and the Family*, Penguin, Harmondsworth, 1970.

LAWRENCE, D. H.: *Women in Love*, Heinemann, London, 1945.

LAWRENCE, D. H.: *Sons and Lovers*, Penguin, Harmondsworth, 1971.

MENNINGER, KARL: *The Crime and Punishment*, Viking Press, New York, 1966.

MEYER, MICHAEL: *Henrik Ibsen*, Rupert Hart Davis, London, 1971.

MISHLER, E. G. and WAXLER, N. E.: *Family Process and Schizophrenia*, Science House, New York, 1968.

MITCHELL, A. R. K.: *Psychological Medicine in Family Practice*, Baillière, Tindall, London, 1971.

MORRIS, NORVAL and HAWKINS, GORDON: *The Honest Politician's Guide to Crime Control*, Chicago University Press, 1970.

NEILL, A. S.: *Summerhill*, Penguin, Harmondsworth, 1968.

Newsweek Magazine: 'Medicine: Help for the Child Beaters', 24 July 1972.

PASAMANICK, BENJAMIN, SCARPITTI, FRANK and DINITZ, SIMON: 'Schizophrenics in the Community', in *Deviance – Studies in the Process of Stigmatization and Societal Reaction*, ed Dinitz, *et al.*, Oxford University Press, 1969.

PITTMAN, FRANK and FLOMENHAFT, KALMAN, 'Treating the *Doll's House* Marriage', *Family Process Journal*, vol. 4, no. 2, June 1970.

ROSZAK, THEODORE: *The Making of a Counter-Culture*, Faber & Faber, 1968.

SANDER, FRED: 'Family Therapy or Religion: A Re-reading of T. S. Eliot's *The Cocktail Party*', *Family Process*, vol. 9, no. 3, September 1970.

SATIR, VIRGINIA: *Conjoint Family Therapy*, Science and Behaviour Books, Palo Alto, California, 1967.

SCHEFF, THOMAS: *Being Mentally Ill*, Aldine, Chicago, 1970.

SEDGWICK, PETER: 'Laing: "Self, Symptom and Society" ' in *Laing and Anti-Psychiatry*, ed Boyers, E. and Orrill, R., Penguin, Harmondsworth, 1972.

SZASZ, THOMAS: 'The Communication of Distress between Child and Parent', in *Theory and Practice of Family Psychiatry*, ed Howells, J. G., Oliver & Boyd, Edinburgh, London, 1968.

SZASZ, THOMAS: *The Manufacture of Madness*, Routledge & Kegan Paul, London, 1971.

SZASZ, THOMAS: *The Myth of Mental Illness*, Paladin, London, 1972.

TESCHER, BARBARA: 'A Nurse, a Family and the Velveteen Rabbit', *Family Process*, vol. 10, no. 3, September 1971.

Time Magazine: 'Education: Who's Retarded?' p. 48.

Time Magazine: 'Behaviour: Mao, the Chinese Freud', 3 July 1972, p. 41.

WATZLAWICK, PAUL, BEAVIN, HELMICK and JACKSON, D.: *The Pragmatics of Human Communication*, Faber & Faber, London, 1968.

WEAKLAND, J. H.: 'The Double Bind Hypothesis of Schizophrenia and Three-party Interaction', in *The Etiology of Schizophrenia*, ed. Jackson, D. D., Basic Books, New York, 1960.

WEBER, MAX: *The Protestant Ethic and the Spirit of Capitalism*, Allen & Unwin, London, 1970.

WILSON, COLIN: *New Pathways in Psychology: Maslow and the Post-Freudian Revolution*, Gollancz, London, 1972.

WOODHOUSE, W. J. and DYNELY, PRINCE: *Encyclopedia of Religion & Ethics*, vol. 11, pp. 218–23.